REPORT

TO THE
SECRETARY OF STATE FOR INDIA IN COUNCIL
ON THE PORTUGUESE RECORDS
RELATING TO
THE EAST INDIES

REPORT

TO THE
SECRETARY OF STATE FOR INDIA IN COUNCIL
ON THE

PORTUGUESE RECORDS

RELATING TO

THE EAST INDIES

CONTAINED IN THE

ARCHIVO DA TORRE DO TOMBO

AND THE
PUBLIC LIBRARIES AT LISBON AND EVORA

F. C. DANVERS

GYAN

Published by

GYAN

Gyan Publishing House
5, Ansari Road
Daryaganj, New Delhi-110002
Phone: 011-47034999, 9811692060
E-mail: books@gyanbooks.com

Distribution Network
gyanbooks.com
India, USA, Canada, UK, Australia, France

ISBN : 978-81-212-4563-0 (HB)
First Published, London, 1892

2nd Impression 2020

Printed at: Gyan Press, Delhi.

REPORT

TO THE

SECRETARY OF STATE FOR INDIA IN COUNCIL

ON THE

PORTUGUESE RECORDS

RELATING TO

THE EAST INDIES,

CONTAINED IN THE

ARCHIVO DA TORRE DO TOMBO,

AND THE

PUBLIC LIBRARIES AT LISBON AND EVORA,

BY

F. C. DANVERS,

REGISTRAR AND SUPERINTENDENT OF RECORDS,
INDIA OFFICE, LONDON.

1892.

REPORT.

My Lord,

In accordance with instructions contained in Council Minutes of the 7th August 1891 and of the 22nd March last, I have made two visits to Portugal for the purpose of inspecting the Records at Lisbon and Evora relating to the early Portuguese possessions in the East Indies. On the former occasion I proceeded to Lisbon by the Royal Mail steamer "*Trent*," which arrived there on the morning of the 12th October, and on the latter I embarked per steamship "*Magdalena*" from Southampton on the 7th April, and reached my destination on the 10th idem. On the occasion of my visit in October of last year I was introduced by Mr. Goschen, Her Majesty's Chargé d'Affaires, to Count Valbom, the Minister for Foreign Affairs, by whom I was most courteously received, and His Excellency kindly explained to me where I should find the records I desired to consult, and gave me a letter to Senhor Lino d'Assumpção, Member of the Board of Management of the Public Libraries and State Paper Office, who afforded me every facility in his power, and for my further assistance introduced me to Senhores José and Raphael Basto, who hold respectively the positions of Director and Conservator of the *Archivo da Torre do Tombo*.

On the 24th October I succeeded, with the kind assistance of Mr. Cowper, the British Consul at Lisbon, in procuring the services of Mr. Henriques, a most experienced linguist, who is repeatedly employed by the Consulate in that capacity. I am much indebted to this gentleman for the very able assistance he rendered me in searching through the Portuguese

Records, many of which, owing to their antiquity, and to their being written in the old style, require an expert to decipher them.

I cannot speak in too great praise of the admirable manner in which the Portuguese Public Records are arranged and preserved. The systematic conservation of the records of the Portuguese nation commenced with the foundation of the monarchy in 1139, and a fixed place for their permanent custody was established in Lisbon during the reign of Dom Diniz, about the commencement of the 14th century. In India a *Torre do Tombo** was established at Goa in 1617, and a similar institution at Salsette in 1620. Although arrangements were thus early made for the proper preservation of the public records, this duty does not appear to have been always performed with equal care and regularity.

In the preliminary notice to Gaspar Correa's "*Lendas da India*," published in 1858, the writer lamented that not one of the treaties concluded with the Kings of Asia, and written upon gold leaf, was then (1858) to be found in the archives. He states that when João de Souza searched the archives for documents in Arabic, which the Academy of Sciences had ordered to be published, he only found 68 in a condition fit for that purpose. One of these, which must have disappeared, is spoken of by the son of Affonso de Albuquerque in the "Commentaries" of his father, of which he was the author, namely the treaty, written on gold leaf and sealed with three golden pendant seals, by which the King of Ormuz declared himself a vassal of the King of Portugal, and bound himself to pay tribute. Even in his own day Braz de Albuquerque evidently entertained some doubts as to the security of this important document, for, after narrating that the treaty, and a copy in the Persian language, enclosed in silver boxes, had been

---

* A "tombo" is an inventory of landed estates and revenues, or, perhaps more strictly, an account of the boundaries and extent of properties.

sent by his father to the King, who had ordered them to be placed in the National Archives, adds, "if by "carelessness this piece of antiquity, so worthy of pre- "servation, have not been already lost." Diogo de Couto also complains, in many parts of his "Decades," of the scandalous carelessness with regard to the title deeds which recorded the history of the achievements of his countrymen and secured rights to the Portuguese Crown.

Early in the present century many miscellaneous loose documents not hitherto properly arranged, or that had been taken out of their places and not put back again, were discovered and formed into separate collections by themselves. It would also appear that from time to time official documents have, for one reason or another, been taken from their proper places in the *Torre do Tombo.* Some of these have since found their way back again into the public archives; such, for instance, as the *Pombal Collection* in the *Bibliotheca Nacional,* and the collection of J. H. de Cunha Rivara at Evora, both of which contain invaluable documents of official origin. It would, however, seem from the gaps that occasionally occur in existing collections, that others may have been similarly removed, which have not yet been returned.

The *Archivo da Torre do Tombo,* together with the *Bibliotheca Nacional,* both of which are under the same management and direction, contain State Records of Portugal up to the year 1833; those of a subsequent date are kept in the several public departments to which they appertain. The *Archivo da Torre do Tombo* also contains the Chronicles of the Kings of Portugal, and the books from several monasteries, which were ordered to be deposited there on the suppression of those institutions in 1834, besides the records of the Inquisition, municipal charters, Papal Bulls, and many other documents of a miscellaneous character, amongst which are several collections relating to the administration of India. These latter I now proceed to describe in fuller detail.

The most important, from an Indian point of view, are the "*Documentos remettidos da India,*" or "*Livros das Monções.*" This series consists of 62 volumes, in which are bound up 12,465 miscellaneous documents received from India, bearing dates between the years 1600 and 1697, and thus covering the whole of the deeply interesting period during which the sovereignty of Portugal in India was being contested by the Dutch and English. This collection is replete with records of the greatest historical importance, and an examination of its contents is rendered easy owing to the existence of two volumes of most carefully prepared tables of contents, affording excellent indications of the subject matter of each document. The first nine volumes of this series, containing documents up to 1616, have been printed *in extenso,* and I have procured copies of these. Volumes 10 and 11 are in course of publication.

The "*Antigo Conselho Ultramarino*" collection of papers may next be noticed. This is contained in the *Bibliotheca Nacional.* It was for many years annexed to the records of the Minister of Marine, some of which documents have apparently got mixed up with these bundles. The *Conselho Ultramarino* to which these papers originally belonged, was founded about the time that the Spaniards were expelled from Portugal, the "*Regimento*" by which it was governed being dated the 14th July 1642. These records are divided into two series, and amongst those in the second series are many important documents relating to India. They are all roughly catalogued and classified under the headings of the different places to which they refer; but there are some bundles still awaiting arrangement, and others merely referred to as "miscellaneous documents." There appear, from the catalogue, to be, in this collection, some documents dated as early as 1544, and they go down to 1834. The *Conselho Ultramarino* was abolished by a decree of the 28th July 1834; documents of a subsequent date, relating to affairs of the foreign possessions of Portugal, have been distributed amongst the different Secretaries of State. The principal documents relating to India in this collection are the letters from the Viceroys, which extend from 1722 to 1833, and are contained in 33 bundles. There are also 32 other bundles of letters from various officers, Bishops, Camaras, &c., relating to India and Macao. The letters from the Viceroys are, unfortunately, not complete. I was unable to find any despatches earlier than 1735, or between the years 1759 and 1765; there are also none for the year 1773, and only one or two for each of the years 1771, 1772, and 1774 to 1776 inclusive, but for the year 1778 there are, in all, 108 despatches now in existence. This collection is, however, on the whole, extremely valuable from an historical point of view, as it contains voluminous records relative to the struggles of the Portuguese with the Mahrattas, and with the Bounsulo, Sunda, and Ponda, their neighbours in the vicinity of Goa, as well as to their alternate wars and negotiations with the once celebrated pirates known as "the Angrias."

Perhaps the next in importance are those records known as "*Corpo Chronologico*." These consist of a miscellaneous collection of 64,376 documents on various subjects, and comprise, *inter alia*, a number of letters and papers relating to India. The period embraced by this series extends from about 1137 A.D. to 1648. The papers relating to India between the years 1500 and 1560 are tolerably numerous; between the latter date and the year 1600 the numbers are proportionately less, but they increase again after the commencement of the 17th century. This collection was arranged by Manoel de Maya, after the earthquake of 1755, from a number of documents he found scattered about in the

Torre do Tombo. It has been most carefully indexed, thus rendering it easy to find those relating to India. Altogether 244 documents were selected as being of sufficient importance to be read through and their contents noted.

The "*Gavetas Antigas*" (old drawers) is a miscellaneous collection consisting of 195 bundles, containing in all 5,274 documents, many of great interest and several relating to India. They are for the most part very old documents, and were collected by Manoel de Maya after the earthquake. They were originally kept in 20 old drawers in the *Archivo da Torre do Tombo*, from which circumstance the name of "*Gavetas Antigas*" is derived. These were all copied into books in 1818 by order of Senhor Francisco Munes Franklin, who was then keeper of the *Torre do Tombo.* The original documents have been carefully indexed, and 68 papers were selected for further examination.

The "*Cartas Missivas*" is a miscellaneous collection, the origin of which is now unknown. It consists of royal decrees and other documents, many of which are, however, without date. These are contained in four bundles, and comprise altogether 1,783 documents, some of which appear to be rough drafts, others are copies, but there are also some original documents and signed letters amongst them. A few of these papers relate to India, but as a rule they are not of much importance. The preservation of most of these documents proves how careful those in charge of the *Torre do Tombo* have been not to destroy anything that might be of value. As these documents are not catalogued or indexed the whole of the collection had to be examined.

The "*Cartas dos Vice Reis da India*" consists of one small packet of 190 documents, ranging in date from the year 1500 to 1584. There is no index, but each document is distinctly numbered and docketed. Some few of them have already been published, others are duplicates of papers in the "*Corpo Chronologico,*" and several are merely copies and undated. Each of these documents had to be examined separately.

The *Pombal Collection* consists of a number of miscellaneous books and documents, mostly MSS., many of which relate to India. It was recently purchased by the State from the Marquis of Pombal, and is now preserved in the *Bibliotheca Nacional.* These documents consist largely of official records; Volume 469 includes a copy of instructions given by the Viceroy, the Marquis de Alorna, to his successor, the Marquis de Tavora, which contain an interesting account of the state of India about the year 1750. This has been separately printed in Goa, and I have been fortunate enough to obtain a copy of it. The papers in this collection are of a most miscellaneous character. There are altogether 297 relating directly to India, some of which are of great historical value. In Volume 611 an account is given of Clive's victories in Bengal.

In the *Academia Real das Sciencias* there are also a few documents scattered amongst its extensive book shelves relating to India, but these did not seem to be of sufficient importance to justify my devoting much time to an examination of them. I shall, therefore, here merely allude to two collections of papers relating to India which were brought specially to my notice, viz.:—1. A MS. book entitled "*Historical Notices about India,*" which consists of diaries, correspondence, and documents of all kinds collected by Dom Manoel Lobe de Sylveira, son of the first Conde de Sarzedas, who lived in India from 1649 to 1708. It commences with a log of Dom Manoel de Sylveira's voyage out to India in the year 1649, and the last document it contains bears date "Baçaim, 30th November 1677." 2. The other work consists of three volumes of letters from the Jesuits in Asia to the head of their Order in Lisbon, and the period embraced in them is from 1544 to 1569 inclusive. Both of these no doubt contain much valuable information regarding events in India during the periods to which they respectively refer, as seen by non-official observers.

Amongst the Portuguese Records relating to India in the *Bibliotheca Nacional* is a MS. work entitled "Descripção das fortalezas da India Oriental" by Pedro Barreto de Rezende. The original of this work is by some said to be that in the Richelieu Library at Paris, from which this copy was made for the Portuguese Government by Donna Christina Garin dos Santos. It contains the portraits of many of the earliest Viceroys of India, with notices of them, as well as plans of the different Portuguese fortresses, accompanied by historical accounts of the same. There is another copy of it in the British Museum; but the work is of such interest and importance from an historical point of view, that it is surprising it has not been published ere this. With the facilities that now exist for making facsimile reproductions this could be done at a comparatively moderate cost. Should its production be undertaken, it would appear to be a work that might be assisted by a subvention from the Literary Grant of this Office.

Barbosa Machado, writing in the last century, states that this book was for some time in the possession of João de Saldanha. Innocençio da Silva, remarked in 1862, that he had seen some MS. notes of José da Silva Costa, stating that the original work had been in his possession. What has become of it now is not known for certain, since some affirm that the book at Paris is a copy and not the original. The original work is supposed to have been finished in 1635, when Rezende was private secretary to the Conde de Linhares, who was then Viceroy of India.

On the 2nd of May, I proceeded with Mr. Henriques to Evora to examine the Portuguese Records there relating to India. These are contained in the Cathedral Library and are under the charge of Senhor A. F. Barata to whom I am much indebted for the very great pains he took to render me every possible assistance in the object of my visit. Here, as at Lisbon, I found that the greatest care has been taken of these Records, and an admirably prepared table of contents renders a search through them a matter of comparative ease. The principal documents relating to India are contained in what is known as the "Rivara Collection." There are, besides, a few other miscellaneous papers bearing on Indian subjects, but these are neither numerous, nor, for the most part, of much importance.

Senhor J. H. de Cunha Rivara was Keeper of the Library at Evora before he went out to India. On the 31st May 1858, he was commissioned by the Portuguese Government to collect all information regarding the history of Portugal in the East. Accordingly he visited the various cities, towns, and places from Dio to Cape Comorin, and from the coast of Malabar to that of Coromandel. The information which he then collected he published in a monthly magazine called "O Chronista de Tissuary," a copy of which I procured in Lisbon. He also published a book entitled "Archivo Portugueze Oriental," which contains copies of many official documents relating to Portuguese possessions in the East. This is now a very rare work, but after many attempts I succeeded in purchasing a complete copy of it. During the progress of his researches and literary works Senhor de Cunha Rivara collected a large number of official records which, at his death, he left to the Public Library at Evora.

For many years past the Portuguese Government have been in the habit of publishing certain of their records, and for this purpose an annual grant is made to the *Academia Real das Sciencias*, which possesses a private printing press. Amongst these are several relating to India, copies of which I have procured. The invariable practice in Portugal, in the publication of their records, is to print all the documents *in extenso*. This, in the present case, is extremely fortunate, since abstracts, however carefully made, would have been practically worthless in this country where it is impossible to refer to the originals in the event of a doubt on any point, or of a desire to see the whole letter.

In the following pages I have given extracts from some of the documents I examined in Lisbon and Evora. These I have, as a rule, arranged in chronological order. Where necessary, in order to make them more intelligible, I have connected them together by brief historical extracts taken from Portuguese publications, and this I have endeavoured to do in such a manner as to avoid any appearance of an attempt to form them into an historical essay, which would have been out of place on the present occasion. It will be observed that my notes end with the concluding years of the 18th century. I advisedly limited my search to that period since, in the request made through the Foreign Office for permission to search the Portuguese State Records relating to India, special reference was made only to those of early date; and, in consequence of reports that were freely circulated about Lisbon as to what was supposed by some to be the real object of my visit, I found it desirable to state distinctly that I should limit my search to documents of the 16th, 17th, and 18th centuries.

I cannot conclude this Report without bearing testimony to the great kindness and assistance I received from everyone with whom I was brought in contact in Lisbon in connection with these duties; and it has been entirely due to the personal interest taken in my work there by the Senhores José and Raphael Basto, at the *Torre do Tombo*, the latter of whom also assisted me at the *Bibliotheca Nacional*, and to Senhor A. F. Barata at Evora, that I have been able to complete my examination in the very short period of about three months of the voluminous documents relating to India, extending over a period of 300 years, that are under their respective charges. I have already referred to the assistance rendered by Mr. G. J. C. Henriques, without whose valuable aid I should have been quite unable to make any practical progress in my search through the Portuguese Records—especially those of earliest date—and finally I desire to record my thanks to Mr. J. L. Chassereau, who has rendered me invaluable aid in the preparation of this Report.

Trusting that the manner in which I have performed the duties entrusted to me may meet with your Lordship's approval,

I have the honour to be,
My Lord,
Your Lordship's obedient Servant,
F. C. DANVERS,
Registrar and Superintendent of Records.

Registry and Record Department,
25th November 1892.

PORTUGUESE INDIA.

SECTION I. 1498—1600.

Vasco da Gama, on his discovery of India, anchored off Calicut* on the 20th May 1498. Calicut was at that time the most important place of trade in the whole of India, and the arrival of the Portuguese there filled the Arabs, then the principal traders to the East, with considerable alarm for the safety of their commerce; they, therefore, did their best to influence the King against them. The intention of the Arabs to prevent the Portuguese from trading direct with India having been communicated to Vasco da Gama, he gave instructions to his Factors that they were to barter their goods for anything the people liked to give in exchange, however worthless or below the proper value it might be. This further incensed the Arabs, who not only ill-treated the Portuguese who went on shore, but also robbed them of their merchandise. Vasco da Gama then left Calicut

* Calicut had been an important emporium of trade from an early date. 'Abd-er-Razzak, in the account of his journey to India about the middle of the 15th century, remarked of Calicut: "In it are to be " found abundance of precious articles brought thither from maritime " countries, and especially from Abyssinia, Zirbad, and Zanguebar; " from time to time ships arrive there from the shores of the House " of God (Mecca) and other parts of the Hedjaz." It is, he says, " a perfectly secure harbour, which, like that of Hormuz, brings together " merchants from every city and from every country." Ibn Batuta describes Calicut as "one of the greatest ports in the district of " Malabar"; Nicolò de Conti as "a maritime city eight miles in circumference, a noble emporium for all India"; and Nikitin says "it is " a very large town, the great meeting place for all nations living along " the coasts of India and of Ethiopia."

and proceeded to Cananor, where he was better received, and having exchanged presents and expressions of friendship with the King of that place, he left India and returned home. Another expedition, under Pedro Alvarez Cabral, was shortly afterwards despatched to India, which anchored before Calicut on the 17th September 1500. Cabral obtained permission from the Zamorin* for the establishment of a factory on the coast, and a treaty† of friendship and commerce was entered into. The factory was peacefully established at Calicut under the direction of Ayres Correa, who took possession of the building with 60 men. Certain merchants of Mecca, however, who had establishments in Calicut, successfully obstructed the Portuguese from obtaining sufficient cargo for their vessels, and only two ships were consequently laden in three months, whereupon complaint was made to the Zamorin, who, however, gave no redress. Shortly afterwards an attack was made on the factory, when Correa and the majority of his company were killed, only a few of them succeeding in reaching the ships. In revenge for this treachery Cabral attacked ten Moorish vessels, which he subsequently burnt. After bombarding the town for two days he proceeded to Cochin, having by the way met with and burnt two more ships belonging to Calicut. Thus was commenced a war of rivalry between the Portuguese and Arabs for the possession of the Eastern trade, in which, at a later date, the natives of different parts of India became involved, accordingly as they encouraged the Portuguese or the Arab traders. In this contest the Venetians gave their support to the Arabs, since the success of the Portuguese could not fail to injure their trade between Cairo and Europe.

---

* The title for many centuries of the Hindu Sovereign of Calicut and the surrounding country; probably a vernacular modification of *Sámundri*, "the Sea-King."—*Yule's Glossary.*

† It does not appear that any copy of this treaty is now on record.

The energy with which the Portuguese hunted down and drove their competitors from the Eastern seas is demonstrated by a letter from Affonso de Albuquerque to the King, dated Goa, 8th November 1512, wherein he said,—

Cartas, p. 98.

"In your Majesty's letters you inform me that over twenty ships sailed last year from Mecca to Calicut with spices. I am not surprised that your Majesty should have been told this, but am indeed astonished that your Majesty should even believe that there exist twenty ships along the whole coast of Malabar. Do not fear Calicut. There is nothing doing there. The trade with the whole gulf of Ceylon was the one which interfered with your Majesty's interests, because fifty ships at least, laden with everything that can be imagined, sailed every year from Malacca and those parts to Mecca. This is not the case now, I am thankful to say."

At Cochin, Cabral established a factory, and left a staff there to collect lading for the next ships that should arrive.* In the year 1502 a factory was established at Cananor. The Zamorin having joined the Moors in their hostilities against the Portuguese, King Dom Manoel determined to send out another expedition under Affonso de Albuquerque, to build a fortress at Cochin for the protection of the agency and merchandise there. Having effected this, Albuquerque opened up a trade with Quilon, and established a factory there in January 1504. The friendship of the King of Cochin with the Portuguese led to continual hostile acts against him by the Zamorin. The necessity for consolidating the Portuguese power in the East now forced itself upon Dom Manoel, and he therefore determined to send out a Governor to remain for three years in India, with a sufficient force to protect the Portuguese settlements there. The first Governor sent out was Dom Francisco de Almeida, who left Lisbon

* In thus establishing factories, Cabral followed the practice initiated, it is believed, by the Phœnicians, who planted factories or agencies in all lands whither they traded, where they were able not only to dispose of their several cargoes to the best advantage, but to collect the produce of the surrounding districts to be ready for shipment on the return of their fleets.

with a fleet on the 25th March 1505, and on his arrival in India, in the following September, he commenced to erect forts at the different Portuguese settlements, and to levy vigorous war against the Moorish ships. He was succeeded by Affonso de Albuquerque in October 1509, under whom the Portuguese power in the East attained its highest development.

It appears that Timoja,* who had formerly been a pirate, but is now described as Captain of the King of Bisnaga,† persuaded Albuquerque, instead of going to attack the Moors in the Red Sea, as he had intended to do, to fight them in their stronghold in Goa.‡ He represented to him the political disorders at Goa; the intention entertained by the Mahomedans of utilizing that naturally powerful position as a base of extensive operations with a view to the expulsion of the Portuguese from India; the death of "the Çabaio" (Yusaf Adil Shah Savaee), Lord of Goa, and the youth and helplessness of "the Hidalcão" (Idalkhan)§ his son. With the assistance of Timoja, Albuquerque captured Goa, which city he took possession of on the 2nd March 1510. The Çabaio was not, however, dead, but only absent in the interior of the country, whence he returned shortly afterwards and recaptured the city on the 20th May after a siege of 21 days.

---

* "Commentaries of Afonso Dalbuquerque," Vol. 2; "Lendas da India," T. I. and II.; Briggs' "Mahomedan Power in India," Vol. III.; "Kanara Gazetteer," Part II.

† The kingdom of Bisnaga or Narsinga occupied, at one time, nearly the whole of Southern India, except Malabar, and extended from one sea coast to the other. The ancient capital of this kingdom is now known as Vijayanagar, in the Bellary District of Madras.

‡ Goa is believed to be the "Kouba" of Ptolemy. The place is mentioned in Ferishta's history of the Deccan, and is said to have been, in the latter part of the 14th century, a seaport appertaining then, as it did for nearly a century afterwards, to the Kings of Bisnaga. Before the advent of the Portuguese in India, Goa had become a very flourishing place for commerce by reason of the excellence of its harbour.

§ The first King of Bisnaga was Yusaf Adil Shah, and his successor was Ismael Adil Shah; but the Portuguese called him Idalxa or Idalcão.

The letters which Albuquerque must have written to the King informing him of the capture and subsequent loss of Goa have disappeared, neither are copies of them now extant; but in a letter of the 17th October 1510 Albuquerque informed His Majesty of his intention to retake Goa, which place he said was of such importance that it would be impossible to hold India without it. Besides its riches and advantages it was then a source of danger, since it was in the hands of the Turks, who had there a great number of galleys and ships, with which they could do an incalculable amount of damage.

Cartas, p. 21.

In accordance with this intention he prepared another expedition, and commenced an attack on Goa on the morning of the 25th November 1510, recapturing the place on the same day. Albuquerque's letter to the King on this enterprise is also missing, but on the 22nd December he said,—

Cartas, p. 26.

"The letter I wrote to your Majesty about the capture of Goa was dispatched the same afternoon, as I determined to send a ship to Cananor to catch the ships that were loading there, and to instruct them to call here on their way in order to show the natives how great was the power of your Majesty's fleet. In the capture of Goa and its fortress we succeeded better than we expected to do. We killed 300 Turks in the place, besides whom numbers of the enemy were drowned in their flight across the river. After this I destroyed the city and put every one to the sword. For the space of four days we spared not a single Moor, and we fired their Mosques; but we spared the Brahmins. The total number of Moors slain, both men and women, amounted to over 6,000. Some of the principal natives from whom the Turks had taken their possessions came up to our help on hearing of the destruction of Goa, and, taking possession of the roads leading from the city, gave no quarter to the fugitives. My plans now are not to allow a single Moor to enter Goa, and, leaving a few ships there, to proceed to the Red Sea."

Probably one of the most interesting documents, from an administrative point of view, in the *Archivo da Torre do Tombo* is the original "*Foral,*" or Regulations for the Land and other Revenue Settlements for Goa, which bears date the 16th September 1526. In the *Bibliotheca Nacional* is also the actual settlement of Salsette and Goa for the year 1607. From the former of these documents it appears that on the 16th September 1526 an investigation was held, by order of the King of Portugal, with the view of fixing a land revenue system for the island of Tiçoare. It comprised in all 31 villages, and each village had a certain number of "gancars" or head men. The principal town of Tiçoare was Goa, which has since given its name to the island. There was a tradition amongst the inhabitants that in ancient times four men had taken possession of the island, then entirely desert; they improved and fortified it, and the population increased in a short time to such an extent that the island became entirely peopled and sent out colonies to the neighbouring lands. Owing to the talent which these people possessed for improving and governing they were called "gancars." Later on, their lands were invaded by the people of neighbouring regions, and these, being of a more warlike nature, subjugated them and forced them to pay tribute or rental in proportion to the lands they occupied.

Gavetas, 20, Maço 10, No. 13.

After investigating the question of existing revenues, the committee appointed for the above purpose proceeded to fix the rent for each village in the following manner. The "gancars" or head men were annually called together by the head "Tanadar"* who informed them of the amount which each village was required to pay to the imperial revenues during the ensuing twelve months; the "gancars" then fixed the amount payable by each cultivator, basing their calculations upon a percentage† of the gross produce. When the receipts from

* The first person who held this office of "Tanadar," to whom I have found reference made in the Portuguese records, was João Machado, who in 1515 was appointed Tanadar at Goa to receive taxes and tributes.

† What this percentage was is not stated.

this assessment were in excess of the estimated sum—as it might be in a year of good crops—any surplus derived therefrom was to be devoted to local improvements, but in the event of their falling short of the required amount, an additional tax had to be imposed by the "gancar" to make up the deficiency. In the event of any village becoming a defaulter to the State, the lands and personal property of the "gancar" were made liable for the full amount due.

Concelho Ultramarinho, Livro 346.

In a *foral* of the district of Salsette* early in the 17th century, it is stated that its name originated from the fact that it contained 66 villages;† that the lands there were very fertile and well cultivated, but on coming under Portuguese rule many of the inhabitants fled across the frontier to adjoining Native States in consequence of the persistent efforts made to convert them to Christianity. Thence they organized attacks upon the new holders of their lands. In addition to the land tax, here called a "*foro*,"‡ several other revenues were collected, including taxes on palm trees, on fisheries, on mines for precious stones, and on various industries. Customs duties were collected at the several ports, usually at rates equal to 7 per cent. *ad valorem* on both imports and exports, but grain paid only 1 per cent., with the exception of rice, upon which no duty was levied. There was also an inland customs line, and in an old picture of the 16th century, in the *Bibliotheca Nacional*, custom houses are represented all round the land boundaries of the districts of Bardes,

* Salsette forms part of the Goa territory, which comprises the districts of Salsette, Goa, and Bardes.

† In Yule and Burnell's Glossary of Anglo-Indian Colloquial Words and Phrases, it is stated that "the name 'Salsette' appears to be the "corruption of a Mahratti name *Sháshti* from *Sháshashti*, meaning "sixty-six." It is also there stated that "the old name of the Island "of Goa, '*Tiçoari*,' means *Tís-wádi*, or 30 hamlets."

‡ This word "*foro*" is supposed to be the origin of the name "*foras*" given to certain lands of Bombay.

Goa, and Salsette, in the vicinity of each ghaut leading from the interior into Portuguese territory.

The capture of Goa by Albuquerque had such an effect upon the Zamorin, that he sent an embassy offering terms of friendship with the Portuguese and a site in Calicut for the erection of a fortress. It soon, however, became clear that he was not in earnest, and Albuquerque accordingly addressed himself* to that king's brother, who was a devoted servant of the King of Portugal. He, at Albuquerque's suggestion, had his brother poisoned, and succeeded him on the throne. There was then no difficulty in securing a site in Calicut for the erection of a fortress, which gave the Portuguese great facilities for trade; and writing to the King on the 30th November 1513, Albuquerque stated—

Cartas, p. 151.

"The Kings of Cochin and Cananor, and the Moors of both kingdoms, complain that the peaceful arrangements between the Portuguese and the Zamorin are prejudicial to their interests."

Under date the 11th December 1513, the King of Cochin addressed a letter to Dom Manoel on this subject, in which he remarked,—

Tratados, T. 1, p. 10.

"I look upon Cochin as belonging to your Majesty as much as Lisbon does, and I have no friend in the whole world like your Majesty. Now I hear that a treaty of peace has been arranged with Calicut by Dom Garcia, who sent presents to the King of Calicut, who in his turn gave him a place to erect a fortress. Now all the merchants from Calicut to this place, who used to come to me for permits to trade, will obtain them at Calicut from your Majesty's Captain."

On the 24th December of the same year a treaty was concluded with the Zamorin under which the King agreed to supply the Portuguese with all the spices and drugs the land produced, for the purpose of lading their ships. Besides favourable terms of duty and facilities for their shipping, it was stipulated that in case of any war the

Tratados, T. 1, p. 21.

* Commentaries of Afonso Dalbuquerque, Vol. IV., p. 72.

King might engage in (provided it was not against a friendly power) the Portuguese would help him; whilst he, the King, undertook to help them with men on the same condition should occasion arise. The revenue of the land was to be equally divided between the King of Calicut and the King of Portugal. The Portuguese were to pay for all the pepper, &c., purchased by them in kind, but the duties thereon in coin.

Cartas, p. 248.

On the same day that this treaty was made Albuquerque addressed a letter to King Dom Manoel informing him that the King of Calicut was sending ambassadors and spices to Portugal, and he pointed out the advisability of giving the ambassadors a grand reception, and of continuing on peaceful terms with their King. He also stated that the King had said if the King of Portugal wished to build ships, &c., there was plenty of cheap wood in his river and port of Chalea which was at his disposal for that purpose.

Tratados, T. 1, p. 33.

Albuquerque was succeeded as Governor by Lopo Soares de Albergaria in 1515, who, in the following year, concluded a Treaty with the King of Quilon, dated 25th September, by which the latter agreed to rebuild, at his own expense, in the same style and in the same place where it had formerly stood, the Church of S. Thomé, and to endow it with the same revenues as it originally possessed. He also further promised to favour and protect the Christians as heretofore; to pay 500 bahars of pepper in three yearly instalments; to let the Portuguese have all the pepper and other spices they might require at the same prices as they paid for them at Cochin, and to export no drugs or spices without their consent. In case of war with a common enemy each party agreed to assist the other. No ships from Quilon were to enter the Straits of Aden, beyond Cape Guardafui, unless in the service of the Portuguese; and any of the King's subjects, whether natives or Moors, who might desire to become Christians were to be at full liberty to do so. Another Treaty on much the same lines as above was subsequently concluded on the 17th November 1520, with the Queen of Quilon, in which it was stipulated that all the pepper in the land was to be sold to the King of Portugal and to nobody else.

Tratados, T. 1, p. 38.

Amongst the documents known as the "*Gavetas Antigas*" in the *Torre do Tombo* are a number of very important papers relative to an inquiry held in Portugal, in August 1523, to prove that the islands of Maluco (the Moluccas) and Banda were discovered by the Portuguese immediately after Affonso de Albuquerque took Malacca in the year 1511, and that they had already been for eight years subject to the King of Portugal when Ferdinand de Magellaẽs set out from Spain. From the document quoted in the margin, it appears that Affonso de Albuquerque despatched from Malacca two ships and a junk, under the command of Antonio de Abreu. One ship was lost, but the crew were taken on board de Abreu's vessel. The latter went to Banda, but the junk proceeded to Maluco, where it was lost and the crew were taken prisoners. Subsequently other vessels went and traded with these islands, and treaties are stated to have been made with their respective Kings by which the latter owned themselves to be vassals of Portugal. But Spain claimed these islands by virtue of their discovery by Magellaẽs' expedition, and the Spaniards established themselves at Tidor, whence, however, they were turned out, in 1529, by Dom Jorge de Meneses, the Portuguese Governor of Ternate. This led to negotiations between the Spanish and Portuguese on the subject, and Commissioners were appointed on both sides to discuss the subject, the result being that a Treaty was concluded at Saragossa, on the 22nd April 1529, by which Spain

Gavetas, 13, M. 6, D. 1.

Tratados, T. 1, p. 45.

sold her rights in those islands to Portugal for a sum of 350,000 ducats of gold.

It is not intended, in the present Report, to follow in detail the adventurous deeds of the Portuguese through the 16th century, during which they were, step by step, acquiring possessions and building up a commercial and military power in the East. The records now extant relating to that period are not very voluminous, but the histories by Castanheda, de Barros, de Couto, Gaspar Correa, and Faria-y-Souza very fairly relate the principal events of the century. The Portuguese records of the 17th and 18th centuries are more numerous, and naturally possess a greater interest for this country than those of earlier date; I shall therefore endeavour to give, in this Report, tolerably full extracts from such of them as relate to events that have been only partially referred to in, or altogether omitted from, existing histories of India.

When Portugal fell under the dominion of Philip II. of Spain, in 1580, the jurisdictions of the two crowns of

MSS.

Spain and Portugal were kept separate and distinct, and for the purposes of administration a Portuguese Council sat at Madrid, and a Council of Regency at Lisbon, by both of whom orders were sent out to India, those from Madrid bearing the signature of the King, and those from Lisbon the sign manuals of the Regents. At the time of the union of the two crowns, the principal fortresses in the East subject to the Portuguese Government were Diu, Damão, Goa, Baçaim, Chaul, Onor, Barcelor, Mangalor, Cananor, Cranganor, Columbo, Cochin, Coriate, Calaiate, Ormuz, Malacca, Ternate, Tidore, Amboino, Solor, Timor, and Macao. The Governments of the several dependencies were kept distinct, Spaniards being exclusively appointed to those positions which belonged to Spain, and, in accordance with the promise made by Philip II. to the Cortes of Thomar, Portuguese only were nominated to those which had been Portuguese territories. To such an extent was this distinction observed that trade between the Portuguese settlement in Macao, and the Spanish settlements in the Philippines was actually forbidden; although when the Dutch began to grow powerful in the Indies, the King decreed that it would be to the interest of both crowns that the Spanish and Portuguese forces in the East should unite in order to drive them out of Formosa. When, however, peace was concluded between Spain and England, in 1604, the Council of Regency at Lisbon decided that the terms of the Treaty should not extend to India; but that "as India had been gained "by the sword, by the sword should it be defended."

Owing to the pressing demands on the finances of Spain, in consequence of her fruitless attempts to bring the Netherlands to submission, the profits of the Indian trade were all absorbed in that enterprise, and the means were absolutely wanting to provide cargoes for the Indian fleets. Up to this time the monopoly of commerce had rested with the Government, but in 1587 the trade with India was handed over to a Company called "Companhia Portugueza das Indias Orientas." This, however, attained to but very small influence, owing to its operations having been always impeded by the Viceroys and other local officials, and it soon came to an untimely end. In consequence of the falling off in the trade with India after the appearance of the Dutch and English vessels in the Eastern seas, the King of Spain determined to imitate the manner in which these conducted the traffic, and accordingly by Royal Decree of the 15th March 1630 he established a Company of Commerce, towards which he himself subscribed 1,500,000 cruzados, at the same time expressing a hope that the public would contribute an equal sum. Circular letters on the subject were sent to the several Camaras throughout Spain and Portugal, and the King addressed a despatch to the Viceroy desiring that encouragement should be given towards the subscription of capital in India, on the ground that the establishment of the proposed Company would tend

MSS.

to weaken the power of their European enemies in the East. Notwithstanding this high patronage, it received support from not one private person, and only a few municipal bodies subscribed towards the undertaking. Consequently, after a brief and unimportant existence, it completely failed in its object and was abolished by Royal Decree of the 12th April 1633, when the State took over its assets and liabilities.

D. R., Livro 32, fol. 47.

In 1635 proposals were made for the establishment of a Company to trade with China, and to this end encouragement was to be given to the inhabitants of India to start private merchant vessels, so as to avoid capture by European enemies. This, however, does not appear to have commended itself to the people of India, and nothing was therefore effected towards the object in view. Formerly, the native traders had been asked by the Company of Commerce to send merchandise to Europe in their vessels, but they had declined on the ground that owing to the manner in which the Company's ships were fitted out, the danger of their being lost was almost certain. As the Company had now ceased to exist, the King expressed a desire to the Viceroy that an attempt should be made to induce them to ship merchandise in the Royal fleets. However, on the proposal that the people of India should thus embark in commerce being laid before the merchants of Goa, they stated that the thing was now impossible since the trade of the country was carried on in war vessels, and that it was by the ruin of the people that the enemies had become rich.

D. R., Livro 32, fol. 96.

D. R., Livro 35, fol. 105.

On the 16th December 1642, a Royal Decree was issued declaring commerce in India to be free, and trade was opened to Portuguese subjects in all articles with the single exception of cinnamon, which was still reserved as a Royal monopoly.

D. R., Livro 48, fols. 109 and 338.

D. R., Livro 54, fol. 208.

In order to still further encourage private enterprise in commerce it was decreed, with the sanction of the Holy See, that all property of commercial men employed in their business should be exempt from sequestration and confiscation, in the event of the owners being condemned by the inquisition for crimes over which it exercised particular jurisdiction; always provided that they did not die impenitent or unconverted, and that the property passed from them to Catholics. All this, however, appears to have been of no avail, for in a letter of the 4th March 1653, the Viceroy reported that commerce had then entirely ceased, and the revenues of the Custom House at Goa had been reduced to a mere nothing.

D. R., Livro 61, fol. 300.

D. R., Livro 56, fol. 489.

Another Company of Commerce was established by Royal Decree of the 16th March 1697, which had an office in Goa. In a letter of the 20th March, the King remarked that it being of convenience that this Company should not be prejudicial, but rather beneficial, to the poor of the city, it should be required to contribute to their assistance to the extent of 60,000 xerafins. It appears that the Company offered to supply 20,000 cruzados for the repair of the royal ships, in addition to a sum of 33,000 cruzados which they had to supply to Mozambique; and in a letter of the 15th March 1697, the King ordered that the former amount should be increased to 50,000 cruzados. In reply, the Viceroy stated he had done all he could to carry out this order, but without success; not, he remarked, that there was no desire on the part of the Company to obey, but because it was considered necessary for the common good that funds should be provided for the erection of new fortresses, which the King had desired to have constructed on the rivers. This amount was accordingly subsequently reduced to 20,000 cruzados. When first started few seem to have taken any interest in the Company, but in 1698 it

Pombal MSS. 439, fols. 208, 210, 211.

appears, from a letter from Goa of that year, to have been engaged in trade with the north, the south, and with China. This Company ceased to exist on the 14th March 1701, on account of the loss of Mombaça, where it had its principal trade.

In 1743 a Frenchman named Cleland endeavoured to start in Lisbon a commercial company for trade with India, in which he seems to have been unsuccessful. The Conde da Ega, who was Viceroy from 1756 to 1767, in many letters to the King lamented the decadence of the Portuguese trade with India. This trade he endeavoured to stimulate by encouraging native manufactures in Goa, which had been allowed to die out, and to that end he introduced native artisans from Tanna, Surat, and Cambay. He also introduced the cotton plant into Goa. As an additional stimulus he advocated grants from the Treasury, and the provision of a ship of war for the transport of merchandise. He also proposed the establishment of a Company for Bengal on similar lines to the one then existing at Goa. This Company was subsequently started, but it enjoyed only a brief existence, and was, before long, ordered by the King to be wound up.

Concelho Ultramarinho, No. 32.

The strained relations between England and Spain, which arose after the accession of Elizabeth to the English throne, led ultimately to a suspension of diplomatic relations in 1584; and the assistance given by Elizabeth to the Netherlands in their revolt against Spanish dominion further aggravated the bad relations between the two countries, so that war became, sooner or later, inevitable. The great preparations for the Spanish Armada, which was directly levied at England, fully justified the naval hostilities against Spain and her foreign possessions by Sir Francis Drake and others. A large Portuguese carack, named the "S. Filippe," having left the rest of the fleet and started for Lisbon from Mozambique in December 1587, encountered, off the Azores, the English Francis Drake with nine vessels, which the Captain (Vendo João Trigueiros) immediately fought, but after an engagement of several hours the "S. Filippe" was captured and taken to England with its crew, and a very rich cargo.*

The "Madre de Dios,"† another Portuguese vessel that was captured by the English, left Lisbon for India

---

* "Da Asia." Dec. X., cap. ix.

The following account of the capture of the "S. Filippe" is given in Hakluyt. "With the consent of the Chief of the Company, Drake "shaped his course toward the Isle of the Azores, and passed towards "the Isle of Saint Michael; within 20 or 30 leagues thereof, it was his "good fortune to meet with a Portugal carak, called 'Saint Philip,' "being the same ship which in the voyage outward had carried the "three Princes of Japan, that were in Europe, into the Indies. This "carak without any great resistance he took, bestowing the people "thereof in certain vessels well furnitured with victuals, and sending "them courteously home into their country; and this was the first "carak that ever was then coming forth of the East Indies; which the "Portugals took for an evil sign, because the ship bare the King's "own name. The riches of this prize seemed so great unto the whole "Company (as in truth it was) that they assured themselves every man "to have a sufficient reward for his travel; and thereupon they all "resolved to return home for England, which they happily did, and "arrived in Plymouth the same summer with their whole fleet, and "this rich booty, to their own profit and due commendation, and to the "great admiration of the whole kingdom. And here by the way it is "to be noted that the taking of this carak wrought two extraordinary "effects in England: first, that it taught others, that caraks were no "such bugs but that they might be taken (as since indeed it hath fallen "out in the taking of the 'Madre de Dios,' and firing and sinking of "others); and, secondly, in acquainting the English nation more "generally with the particularities of the exceeding riches and wealth "of the East Indies, whereby themselves and their neighbours of "Holland have been encouraged, being men as skilful in navigation "and of no less courage than the Portugals, to share with them in the "East Indies, where their strength is nothing so great as heretofore "hath been supposed."

The value of the cargo of the "S. Filippe" was 108,049*l.* 13*s.* 11*d.*—*Calendar of State Papers, Domestic*, 1581–1590, p. 428.

† "Da Asia," Dec. XI., cap. xiv. According to the account in Hakluyt, the English fleet, under Sir John Burrough, caught sight of the "Santa Cruz" off the Isle of Flores, and gave chase, whereupon it was run ashore and set on fire. About a month afterwards, on the 3rd August, "Capt. Thomson, in the 'Dainty,' had first sight of the

on the 4th April 1589, under the command of Captain Bernardino Ribeiro Pacheco, accompanied by four other vessels. Four of this fleet started on their homeward voyage on the 10th January 1592. The "Bom Jesus," in which was the Governor Manoel de Souza Coutinho, was lost at the entrance to Mozambique with all on board; another of the vessels, the "S. Bartholomeu," was never more heard of; the "Madre de Dios" and the "Santa Cruz" arrived in the neighbourhood of the island of Terceira, where they encountered seven English vessels, which captured the flagship, and took it with all on board to England. The "Santa Cruz," being nearer the coast, was run on shore by its captain and set on fire, to prevent it from falling into the hands of the English. There was another vessel named the "Madre de Dios" afterwards built at Bassein, which started for home in January 1595, and was lost off Socotra.

Towards the end of the sixteenth century the Moors fitted out piratical fleets to prey upon the commerce of the Portuguese and their allies, and foremost

---

" huge carak called the 'Madre de Dios,' one of the greatest receit, " belonging to the crown of Portugal. The 'Dainty,' being of ex- " cellent sail, got the start of the rest of our fleet, and began the conflict " somewhat to her cost, with the slaughter and hurt of divers of her " men. Within a while after Sir John Burrough, in the 'Roebuck' " of Sir W. Raleigh's, was at hand to second her, who saluted her with " shot of great ordinance, and continued the fight within musket shot, " assisted by Capt. Thomson and Capt. Newport, till Sir R. Crosse. " vice-admiral of the fleet, came up, being to leeward, at whose arrival " Sir J. Burgh demanded of him what was best to be done, who " answered that if the carak were not boarded she would recover " the shore and fire herself as the other had done. Whereupon " Sir J. Burgh concluded to entangle her; and Sir R. Crosse promised " also to fasten himself to her together at the instant; which was per- " formed; but after a while Sir J. Burgh, receiving a shot with a " cannon piece under water and ready to sink, desired Sir R. C. to fall " off, that he might also clear himself, and save his ship from sinking, " which with difficulty he did; for both the 'Roebuck' and the " 'Foresight' were so entangled as with much ado could they clear " themselves. The same evening Sir R. Crosse, finding the carak then " sure and drawing near the island, persuaded his company to board

amongst these piratical Chiefs was Kotakkal Kunhali Marakkars,—commonly called the Kunhali,—who had established himself in a fortress at the mouth of the Kota river, on the Malabar coast. In order to destroy this fortress, a Treaty was concluded, in December 1599, between André Furtado de Mendonça and the King of Calicut, in accordance with which the latter was to supply, as long as necessary, 1,000 workmen for the camp and siege, and 15 elephants as long as the siege lasted; to provide all the necessary timber, carpenters, sawyers, &c.; to find 5,000 men-at-arms for the siege, to supply four ships with sailors and lascars to watch and protect the river, besides 30 smaller boats for the same purpose; and 200 axes and 1,000 baskets for the siege. André Furtado on his part undertook that directly the fort of Kunhali should be captured it would be destroyed, and the King would receive half the money, goods, and artillery found in the place, whilst all other arms discovered there were to be the property of the finders. The King also undertook to erect a Church and Factory in Calicut. The attack was made and the fort was captured and destroyed; Kunhali was taken and carried to Goa, where he was condemned to death as a traitor to his King, a pirate, and a persecutor of the Christians, and he was accordingly beheaded, together with many of his companions.*

Tratados, T. I., p. 186.

" her again, or else there was no hope to recover her; who, after many " excuses and fears were by him incouraged, and so fell athwart her " foreships all alone, and so hindered her sailing that the rest had time " to come up to his succour, and to recover the carak ere she recovered " the land; and so toward the evening, after he had fought with her " alone three hours single, my lord of Cumberland's two ships came " up, and with very little loss entered with Sir R. Crosse, who had in " that time broken their courages, and made the assault easy for the " rest.".

* " Da Asia," Dec. XII., Cap. 7, 8, and 11.

PORTUGUESE INDIA.

SECTION II. 1600—1650.

The commencement of the 17th century found the Portuguese power in India already rapidly on the decline. It had reached its climax about the year 1571. Shortly afterwards it was decided to divide the Eastern possessions of Portugal into three governments;* D. Antonio de Noronha was appointed Governor of all territories between Cape Guardafui and the island of Ceylon; Antonio Moniz Barreto of those between Pegu and China; and Francisco Barreto of the eastern coast of Africa. This subdivision of authority is held by many to have had a very detrimental effect upon the Portuguese power, but the change of circumstances that followed the subordination of Portugal to Spain had much more serious consequences. The Indian revenues were absorbed by Spain in her struggles with the Netherlands, and the obstructions put in the way of the Dutch trade with Lisbon—which was entirely prohibited in 1598—led the latter to go direct to India for that commerce they had hitherto been content to obtain only at second hand in Lisbon, and which had greatly enriched that country. The success of this enterprise led the English to follow suit, and the commencement of the 17th century thus brought two rivals to share with Portugal the riches of the Eastern trade.

The following account from Portuguese sources of a remarkable man, who is referred to in English histories of Burma, will not be out of place in this Report:

* "Ensaios," p. 25.

Salvador Ribeiro de Souza* was one of the many Portuguese soldiers of fortune who at the beginning of the 17th century used to render their services to the Kings of the small states into which "Chinese India" was, at that time, divided. Born at Guimarães he, towards the close of the 16th century, went to Arakan, where he obtained a captaincy in the native forces. Associated with him in the command was Filippe de Brito Nicote, a native of Lisbon, but of French nationality, a man as ambitious as de Souza was disinterested. The King of Arakan granted them permission in 1600 to establish a Factory and Custom House at Sirião.† Nicote, thereupon, thinking that he would make a better bargain by offering this concession to the Portuguese Government to act as a starting-point for fresh conquests, set out for Portuguese India in order to carry out this design, leaving Salvador Ribeiro de Souza at Sirião. The King of Arakan, filled with indignation at Nicote's proceedings, ordered all the Portuguese to be expelled from his kingdom, and for that purpose collected an army of 40,000 men and a fleet of 1,200 sail. De Souza, with a handful of his fellow countrymen, retired to their fortress, which they defended most heroically, finally routing the natives in a nocturnal sally and causing the siege to be raised. The fame of this action spread over the neighbouring kingdoms, and made such an impression upon the inhabitants of Pegu that they resolved to offer the crown of their country to this valiant warrior. De Souza accepted it, and reigned for some time over Pegu. Nicote, meanwhile, having alleged great services to the Portuguese Government, was named Captain General of all he could conquer in those

D. R., 1613, Maço 15, Doc. 352.

---

* "Alemquer e seu Concelho," p. 211. Also "Ensaios," p. 27; "History of Burma," by Lieut.-General Sir Arthur P. Phayre, p. 125; and British Burma Gazetteer.

† Syriam, more correctly called Than-lyeng, is a town in the Rangoon district of the Pegu Division, on the left bank of the Pegu river, about three miles from its mouth.

parts. When he appeared at Pegu, de Souza resigned to him the crown with which he had been invested, and retired to Portugal, where he is supposed to have passed the remainder of his days at his native village in the province of Minho; but his body lies in the chapter house of a small Franciscan convent near Alemquer, some 30 miles from Lisbon, where an inscription records his name and history. Portuguese writers call him the Marcus Aurelius of the Decadence of India, and more than one poet has sung his praises.

D. R., 1613, Dec. 20, Doc. 397.

The end of Filippe de Nicote is worth recording. The rank which he so ungratefully and so meanly obtained was fatal to him. Power and ambition made him a tyrant, while riches and the slothful splendour of oriental life caused him to become enervated and negligent. In 1613 the King of Ava surprised his fortress, and Nicote was impaled upon the ramparts, whilst his son, who had married a daughter of the King of Martaban, was assassinated by his father-in-law.

The Dutch made their earliest expeditions to Java and the Eastern Islands, and from the first treated the Portuguese as enemies, levying war upon their ships and possessions, nor was it long before they succeeded in driving them out of Amboina, Tidor, and Borneo. The English, on the contrary, endeavoured to avoid hostilities with the Portuguese, with whose trade, however, they openly competed. The Portuguese designated the former "rebeldes,"* and the latter

---

* The application of the term "rebeldes" to the Dutch can be easily understood, as Holland was at this time in rebellion against the King of Spain, who then also ruled Portugal. I have been unable to discover the origin of the term "piratas" as applied to the English. Their system of maritime commerce at this time was not such as would have been countenanced at a later date, but in this respect they were no worse than the Dutch or the Portuguese themselves. It is a curious fact that during the recent strained relations between England and Portugal the term "piratas" was revived towards the English as a term of contempt. It was also subsequently applied to English sovereigns, which constitute the principal gold currency in Portugal.

"piratas," and wrote of them in their official correspondence in those terms.

The first encounter* between the English and Portuguese occurred in October 1611, but I have been unable to find any description of this in the Portuguese records. Of the next engagement,† which occurred off Swally

---

* In "The Voyages of Sir James Lancaster, Kt., to the East Indies" (Hakluyt Society) the following account is given of this encounter. In the second voyage of Sir Henry Middleton, being the sixth set forth by the East India Company, the fleet anchored off the bar of Surat on the 26th September 1611, but was so closely watched by a Portuguese fleet that neither letters nor provisions could approach the English ships. Strict orders were given by Sir Henry Middleton that no violence should be offered the Portugals unless they were the assailants. Emboldened by this impunity, their frigates used to run very close to the vessels, and at night watch had to be kept against any attempt to surprise the smaller ships. At length the General sent, by a native boat, a letter to the Captain-Major, being a caveat against breaking the peace between their respective Princes, and giving the reasons for his being there. To this letter no answer was returned. The Captain-Major, however, subsequently offered to accompany Sir Henry Middleton to Goa to learn the Viceroy's pleasure, otherwise he could not allow of any business being transacted. In reply Sir Henry requested that if the Captain-Major could not allow him to trade there he would permit Captain Sharpeigh and his companions, who had arrived at Surat from Agra, to join the ship "Trade's Increase"; to which the Portugal answered "No," for he could carry them to Goa, whence they should be sent home. As no fresh provisions could be procured, owing to the watchfulness of the Portugals, for want of which many men fell ill, Sir Henry Middleton forwarded instructions to Captain Sharpeigh to despatch some to the fleet at all risks. This the latter did, but the boat was captured by the Portugals, upon which "in scoffe the Captaine-Major "sent presently thanks unto Captaine Sharpeigh for his care of him in "sending him victuals for his supply." Sir Henry Middleton, on the 12th October, made another attempt to discover a place where the ships could be sufficiently close to the shore to command the landing place with their guns. For this purpose the vessels stood in towards the land; the smaller ones, with their boats ahead taking soundings, being in advance, while the Portugal frigates ever kept in shore of them. The Portugals, emboldened by long immunity, having attempted to cut off the "Darling's" boat, the Master of that vessel opened fire on them; upon which the crew of one frigate, seeing the shot falling around them, ran their boat ashore, and, though the other frigates at first seemed inclined to attempt a rescue, she remained a prize. Thus the peace between the English and Portugals was broken.

† "The 25th of November we received letters from Mr. Canninge and Ed. Christian, wherein they advised us of 4 galleons ready to

in November 1612, between Captain Best and a Portuguese fleet commanded by Captain Major Nuno da Cunha, the only particulars I have found amongst the Portuguese records are given in some English letters sent by the King to the Viceroy in a letter of the 24th February 1615, which it appears were taken from an Englishman who was carrying them home *viâ* Persia, but who died by the way, and these letters fell into the hands of some Portuguese and were by them forwarded to Lisbon. These documents consist of letters addressed to Sir Thomas Smith, the Governor of the East India Company, by Captain

D. R., 1614, Feb. 24, Doc. 445.

---

depart from Goa, on purpose to take or to fire our ships, which proved true, for that the 28th ditto the frigates, in number 25, who came in company with the said galleons to assist them, set Mr. Canninge on shore at the city of Surat, Ed. Christian having escaped from them by their joint consent and plot at Cambaya some 4 days before. The 29th ditto Mr. Canninge repaired aboard, we accompanying him to the water side to see the event of this business, and this afternoon the galleons, with 6 frigates to each of them towing, came near our ships, who also weighed anchor and met them, in sight of us and many other people standing on the shore to look on them, where the 'Dragon' alone, at the first encounter, made their Admiral and Vice-Admiral turn back and fly before her, their other 2 ships not being come up, neither was the 'Ozeander' at this time come to the 'Dragon,' and having exchanged some 40 great shot of each side, the night being come they anchored in sight of each other, and the next morning our ships weighed again, and began their fight with them, which continued some 3 hours; in which time they drove 3 of their galleons on the sands, and so our ships came to an anchor; and in the afternoon weighed again, in which time the flood being come, the galleons with the help of the frigates were afloat again, with whom this third time our ships having fought some 4 hours with much honour and advantage of their enemies, it being now night, came to an anchor, and there rode this night and all the next day without meddling with each other. The 31st ditto our ships set sail and departed, whereupon we much doubted some great hurt to be done aboard them, but thanks be to God it proved contrary, we having had but one man slain in these 3 fights. What passed with them in their fights on the other side, we refer you to their particular letters who were present at them."—*Letter from Thos. Aldworthe, Wm. Biddulph, and Nich. Withington, at Surat,* 25 *January* 1612–13 (O C., 102). *See also Journal of Ralphe Crosse, Hakluyt Society, No.* 56, *p.* 233.

Best, Thomas Keridge (one of the Factors at Surat), Ralphe Crofte (Purser of the "Osiander"), and one from the Rev. Patrick Copland (Minister with Best's fleet) to the Rev. A. Randal, Minister of Saint Andrew's Church, London, together with a copy of a treaty concluded between Thomas Best and the Great Mogul for the establishment of commerce and factories at Surat, Ahmedabad, Cambay, Gogo, and any other part of the territories of the Great Mogul. The particular interest which attaches to these documents is that of the most of them no copies exist among our own records, and this is the case as regards Thomas Best's letter, which contains an account of the engagement above referred to.

The Portuguese were still determined to resist, as far as possible, the establishment of an English Factory at Surat, and it required another sharp lesson before they were brought to recognize the fact that they were not possessed of the power to prevent it, based as the English right was upon a firman granted by the Great Mogul. The feeling of the Portuguese towards the English at this time is clearly shown by a letter from the Viceroy to the King, wherein he wrote of them as,—

> "thieves, disturbers of States, and a people not to be permitted in a commonwealth, and that if the King received them they would never have peace with him, but do him all possible prejudice, threatening to effect some great exploit upon these your ships, and after to take all the seaports."*

An encounter took place between the ships under Nicholas Downton and a Portuguese fleet off Swally in January 1615,† but I have been unable to find any

* This quotation is taken from a letter from Thos. Kerridge to the Company of 20th January 1614–15, in which he adds: "A copy of "this letter I desired to have sent your worships, but could not pro-"cure it, being it was only interpreted to the King, and not translated." —O. C., 235.

† The following particulars are taken from Downton's Journal, which

account of it amongst the Portuguese records. After this the Portuguese concluded a treaty with Jehangir, dated the 7th June 1615, with the view of keeping the English and Dutch out of India, which contained, amongst others, the following conditions :—

Tratados, T. I., p. 189.

" Whereas the English and Dutch, under the guise of merchants, come to these parts to establish themselves here and make conquests of the lands; and whereas their presence in the neighbourhood of India would do a great deal of harm to all, it is now agreed that neither the King Jehanguir or the Viceroy of the State of India shall have any commercial relations with the aforesaid nations, neither shall they give

---

has long ago disappeared from the India Office Records, but has been preserved for us (in brief) in the pages of " Purchas Pilgrimes ":—

" The ships concerned were those of the second voyage on account of the First Joint Stock, viz., the " New Year's Gift," the " Hector," the " Merchant's Hope," and the " Solomon," all under the command of Nicholas Downton. They reached Swally the 15th October 1614, and found the Portuguese at war with the natives. On the 16th December a Portuguese fleet burnt Gogo and a number of native vessels ; and a week later 22 frigates anchored near the English vessels, between them and Surat. Slight skirmishes took place on the 27th and 28th. On the 29th the English fleet sailed and took up a better position at Swally itself, thus getting once more into communication with Surat. On the 14th January 1615, a force of Portuguese vessels made their appearance, and were quickly followed by others, until by the 19th they numbered 8 galleons, 3 lesser ships, and 60 frigates. The Nabob, in great alarm, endeavoured to make terms, but the Portuguese commander held back, hoping, after he had overthrown the English, to have the natives entirely at his mercy. The 20th the " Merchant's Hope " stood towards the enemy, followed shortly afterwards by the other three vessels. The Portuguese ships and frigates, supported by the galleons, which, however, could not come too near because of want of water, closed round the " Merchant's Hope," and boarded her with great resolution. They were repulsed with much slaughter, and their three ships lying alongside the English ship were taken. Before quitting their ships, the Portuguese set them on fire, in hopes to burn the " Merchant's Hope " with them; but the English sailors managed to cast them loose, and they drifted on to the sands, where they burnt out harmlessly. Meanwhile a cannonade was kept up with the galleons until night. This successful resistance encouraged the Nabob to refuse an overture of peace from the Portuguese."

Elkington's letters (O. C., 237 and 238) add a few other particulars

them shelter in their ports nor supply them with provisions. The English now in those parts shall leave them with their goods *viâ* Masulipatam. For the sake of peace and concord all differences between, and all losses, &c., sustained by Moguls and Portuguese, shall be forgotten. From this date they shall be at peace, and the Portuguese shall be at liberty to travel by land and sea to the ports and territories of the King Jehanguir and trade there. In the same way shall the vassals of the said King be at liberty to trade with the ports and territories of the King of Portugal. The King Jehanguir shall release all Portuguese captives who may not have become Moors, the Viceroy to release all subjects of King Jehanguir who may not have become Christians. The Malabars being pirates, who gain their livelihood by theft, shall not be allowed to enter the ports of either King, and should they do so the Portuguese shall be permitted to enter any port or river where the Malabars may happen to be, and seize them. This treaty of peace shall in no wise affect the rights which the King of Portugal has had of demanding dues at Dio from the vessels navigating the bay of Cambaya; on the contrary, he shall maintain the same rights as hitherto."

The internal affairs of the Portuguese in India appear about this time to have been in a very disordered and unsatisfactory condition. Repeated instructions were sent out to the Viceroys from Lisbon, that the money furnished for the purchase of spices should be devoted to the purposes for which it was supplied. This, taken in conjunction with the record of repeated instances of officers in India being heavily indebted to the State, clearly indicates the existence of a considerable amount of peculation. The want of funds in India was evidently very great; and in order to provide means for the proper maintenance and repair of certain forts, it became the custom, when the need was very urgent, to send out vessels, the profits of their respective voyages being devoted in advance to certain specific purposes. The wealth of the convents in India had already been lent to the State, and absorbed in the general expenses of

---

of the fight on the 20th January. They state that when the Portuguese boarded the "Merchant's Hope" they twice nearly succeeded in taking her; and that they lost between 400 and 500 men, amongst them many cavaliers, while the English loss was small.

administration, and at the time when the sinews of war were most urgently required in the struggles of the Portuguese with the English and Dutch, their pecuniary resources were at the lowest ebb. People were encouraged to pay their taxes in copper, and even Chinese copper was accepted at certain ports, in order that the metal might be used in the manufacture of cannon. It was not an unfrequent occurrence for the copper guns to be stolen from the forts wherein they were placed, and several instances occur in the Records of inquiries ordered to be instituted on this account. At last, in 1634, orders were given that the guns should be all cast in iron.

D. R., Livro 17, fols. 23, 170, 172, 174, 187, 210, 211.

In 1623, Dom Francisco da Gama, Conde da Vidigueira, succeeded as Viceroy, and he at once made a close examination into the state of affairs then existing in India. His letters to the King, which are very numerous, are full of interest. He reported that everything in India was in as bad a state as possible; the fortresses were ruined and without guns; Ormuz, which had produced the largest revenues, was lost; Cochin, which used to be the most prosperous settlement, had then hardly any trade, and was almost in a state of ruin, and without any means of defence, whilst the enemies were in great force in the Indian seas. The only thing to be done was, in his opinion, to make peace with the Dutch on any terms, even to allowing them to trade at Portuguese ports. Goa was for some time blockaded by a combined English and Dutch fleet,* which he was without the means of attacking, but they retired from before that place on the 19th March 1623 without assaulting it.

---

* The combined fleet was called the "Fleet of Defence." It consisted of the "Exchange," "Ann," and "Diamond," and four Dutch vessels; they arrived before Goa about January 1623, their object being

Notwithstanding the persistent opposition which the Portuguese Government offered to the establishment of the Dutch in India, it appears that certain individual Portuguese, in various places, traded directly with them, and even ecclesiastics engaged in this illicit traffic, hoping that their position would save them from suspicion. To such an extent does this appear to have been carried on, that it was found necessary to send out orders from home directing that anyone found so offending should be punished. All sorts of means appear to have been adopted in order to increase the legitimate trade, and, amongst others, the wearing of certain head-dresses in India was prohibited, as they interfered with the sale of fine linen.

MSS.

By 1633 the Portuguese were in a worse plight than ever in India. In Ceylon, as well as in other settlements, the natives had risen against them, and the revenues at their different ports had dwindled down to practically nothing. In this year the Viceroy reported the arrival of French vessels in the Indian seas, thus bringing other competitors into the field for a share in the Eastern trade. Further troubles arose from the fact that of the men sent out from Portugal to assist in the defence of their possessions, a large number became monks on their arrival in India, and so escaped the dangers attending the support of a moribund cause. The final blow to Portuguese prestige in India also took place this year, when their settlement of Hugli, in Bengal, was attacked*

D. R., Livro 30, fol. 263.

"to hinder the Portugals of sending any goods this year into Portugal." O. C., 1089, 1099, and 1149.

* The account of this siege given in the "Statistical Account of Bengal," states that "Over a thousand Portuguese were slaughtered, "and upwards of four thousand men, women, and children were made "prisoners of war. Out of more than three hundred vessels of all "sizes, only three made their escape." Vol. III., p. 300.

by the forces of the Mogul Shah Jehan. It was garrisoned by only 200 Portuguese with 600 Christian slaves. This small garrison valiantly defended themselves from the 21st June until the 29th September, when they were at last obliged to yield; the majority of those who remained alive were taken prisoners and carried to Agra, but a few managed to escape and fortified themselves on an island in front of where their former fortress had been, whence they were removed to Goa by an expedition which the Viceroy sent out for that purpose in 1643.

D. R., Livro 30, fols. 281 and 288.

Evora Cod., CV. 2–19, f. 62.

Although a treaty of peace had been concluded between the Crowns of England and Spain on the 15th November 1630, the President of Surat objected to putting it in force. It was argued on the Spanish side that by Article 9 of the Treaty of 1604* the English were not allowed to pass to India, nor carry on commerce in any part of it, and this, it was

Tratados, T. II., p. 2.

D. R., Livro 32, fol. 72. Livro 33, fol. 72.

---

* In the course of the negotiations for this Treaty, the Spanish Commissioners pressed hard for the acknowledgment of the illegality of the English trade with the Indies, but without success. "The "English negotiators proposed that a proclamation should be issued "forbidding English subjects from trading with places actually in the "occupation of the Spanish Government, on condition that Spain "would withdraw all pretentions to exclude them from trading with "the independent natives. They refused, however, to bind themselves "to obtain a written promise from the King that he would prohibit his "subjects from engaging in the contraband trade, and the proposition "was rejected. They contented themselves, as Elizabeth would have "done if she had been alive, with ignoring the whole subject in the "treaty, though they expressed their opinion strongly enough in the "conference." (Gardiner's *History of England*, Vol. I., p. 211.)

Article 9 of the Treaty of 1604 is as follows:—"IX. It was and is "agreed and settled, that there be and ought to be a free commerce "between the said most serene King of Spain and the said most serene "King of England, and between all their vassals, inhabitants and

claimed, was confirmed by Articles 3 to 8 of the Treaty of 1630. Because the English did not trade with India

---

" subjects whatsoever, as well by land as by sea and fresh water, in all " and singular the kingdoms, dominions, and islands, and other lands, " cities, towns, villages, ports, and districts of the said kingdoms and " dominions, *in which commerce was held before the breaking out of " the war, and according to the usage and observance of ancient cove- " nants and treaties before the war;* so that the subjects and vassals " of either king may, without any passport, general or special licence, " come and enter into the said kingdoms and dominions, either by sea, " land, or fresh water, and into the cities, towns, villages, ports, shores, " creeks, and districts thereof, *and enter into any ports in which com- " merce was carried on before the war, and according and agreeably " to the usage and observance of ancient covenants and treaties before " the war*, with waggons, horses, burdens, and ships or boats as well " laded as to be laded; and may import, buy, and sell merchandizes in " the said places, and purchase provisions, and all other things neces- " sary for their journey or voyage at a just price, and endeavour to " restore their own boats and carriages, or those they have hired or " borrowed, and depart from thence with the same liberty, with all " their merchandizes, goods, and things whatsoever, only paying the " present duties and customs according to the statutes of the place, and " go to their own and foreign countries in what manner they please, " and without any lett or impediment." F. O. Library, 4to, No. 3693.

Paragraphs 3 to 8 of the Treaty of 15th November 1630, are as follows:—

III. Nor shall any of the foresaid most serene Kings, their heirs and successors whatsoever, do, act, or attempt any thing either by themselves or others against the other his kingdoms, countries, or dominions whatsoever, in any place, whether by sea, land, fresh water, or in ports, upon any account or for any cause whatsoever, nor consent or join with any one in war, counsel, attempt, or treaty that may be to the prejudice of the other.

IV. That neither of the parties shall give, nor consent that his vassals, subjects, or inhabitants give assistance, favour or counsel directly or indirectly, by sea, land, or fresh water; nor afford, or consent that his said vassals, subjects, or inhabitants afford men, provisions, money, warlike instruments, or any other assistance to foment war, to the enemies and rebels of the other party, of whatsoever kind they be, whether they invade the kingdoms, countries, and dominions of the other, or withdraw themselves from his dominion and obedience.

V. They shall moreover renounce, even as by the tenor of these presents the said Kings shall and do renounce, each of them any league, confederacy, stipulation, or intelligence howsoever made in prejudice of the one or the other, that is or may be repugnant to the

when other treaties were in existence, the King of Spain called on the King of England to withdraw all

---

present peace and agreement, and all and singular the contents thereof; and they shall annul and make void for the foresaid effect, all and every one of these, and declare them to be of no effect or moment.

VI. It is covenanted and agreed, that the said most serene Kings shall order their subjects to abstain from all manner of force and injury; and shall revoke all manner of commissions and letters of reprisal and mark; and all such as contain a power of plundering, of whatsoever kind or condition they be, that are given and granted to their subjects, inhabitants or foreigners, in prejudice of either of the Kings or of their subjects; and shall declare them null and void, even as they are by this Treaty of Peace declared null and void. And whosoever contravene it shall be punished, and besides criminal punishment inflicted, shall be compelled to make full damages to the aggrieved subjects.

VII. It was and is agreed and settled, that there be, and ought to be a free commerce between the most serene King of Spain and the most serene King of Great Britain, and all their vassals, inhabitants, and subjects, as well by land as by sea and fresh water, in all and singular the kingdoms, dominions and islands, lands, cities, towns, villages, ports, and districts of the said kingdoms and dominions, where commerce and trade was carried on between the said kingdoms before the war between Philip II., king of Spain, and Elizabeth, Queen of England, as it was settled in the Treaty of Peace in the year 1604, Article IX., according and agreeably to the use and observance of ancient covenants and treaties preceding the said time; so that without any passport, general or special licence, either by land, sea, or fresh water, the subjects and vassals of both Kings may go, enter, and sail to all the foresaid places, and all their cities, towns, and ports, shores, coasts, and districts, and enter into any ports in which there was a mutual commerce before the said time; and according and agreeably to the ancient custom and usage of ancient covenants, and of the said treaties, may import merchandizes upon waggons and horses, in carriages and boats loaded or to be loaded; buy and sell in the said places as much provision as will be necessary for their sustenance, journey, or voyage, and purchase them at a reasonable rate; and take care to return their own hired or borrowed ships or wagons; and with the same liberty depart from thence with all their merchandizes, goods, and things whatsoever, paying only the present toll and duty according to the statutes of the places, and from thence go to their own foreign countries, as they please, without any impediment or hindrance.

VIII. It was and is likewise agreed and settled, that it shall be lawful to go to the ports of the said Kings, there remain, and depart from thence with the same liberty, not only with merchant ships, but also with all manner of ships of war, prepared to repulse the attacks of his vessels from India and not to allow any more to go there. An agreement* was, however, entered into at Goa, between the Portuguese Viceroy, the Conde de Linhares, and William Methwold, President of the East India Company in India, on the 20th January 1635, wherein it was stipulated that there should be a cessation of arms between the two nations in India and a union of them against the common enemies,—

Tratados, T. II., p. 52.
D. R., Livro 45, fol. 277.

"by which the subjects of both shall not only increase in their States, but also both Kings in their renown. His Excellency having seen and considered of this just proposition, and oftentimes communicated the same to his Council, resolved to condescend to that proposition so and in such manner as it was capitulated between the Kings of England and Spain in Madrid the 15th of November, anno 1630, without addition or diminution, or giving any other sense to any other thing that is not conformable to that peace notwithstanding it shall be understood that there shall be a truce and cessation of arms until such time as the most illustrious Kings of England and Spain shall declare reciprocally themselves, each to other, that they are not pleased therewith, and it shall so continue six months after such notice shall be given unto the said Viceroy of India and the President for the English nation then being in India, that so the merchants may have time to withdraw and retire their merchandizes, &c."

When the English President in Surat went to Goa to arrange the armistice he agreed to exchange copper with the Portuguese for pepper.

D. R., Livro 34, fol. 3.
" " 44, fol. 152.

---

the enemy, whither they shall be driven by the violence of storm, or to mend their ships, or to buy provisions; provided that if they come in freely and of their own accord, they do not exceed the number of six or eight ships, and do not remain longer in the ports or about the ports, than shall be necessary for refitting or purchasing necessaries lest they should be a hindrance to the free commerce of other friendly nations. But if there shall be a greater number of ships of war, then they shall not come in without first consulting the King, and provided they commit no hostility in the said ports in prejudice of the said Kings, but live and be at rest like friends and confederates. F. O. Library, 4to, No. 3693, p. 281.

* This document does not exist amongst the India Office Records, but the subject is referred to in O. C. 1543 B.

and the Viceroy subsequently reported that he was by this means obtaining copper at lower prices than it could be procured elsewhere. But in December 1638 the King expressed his disapproval of this transaction, and ordered it to be discontinued.

D. R., Livro 33, fol. 71.

After the conclusion of the armistice we find it reported that the Portuguese in Surat were living on good terms with the English, and an arrangement was come to between them that the latter were to be allowed to ship pepper free from opposition by the former, from whom, however, they were to buy it instead of from the natives.

D. R., Livro 33, fol. 247.

Owing to the want of ships, the Portuguese Viceroy (Conde de Linhares) chartered an English ship from the President at Surat for a voyage to China,* a proceeding which was, however, very adversely commented on by his successor.

D. R., Livro 33, fol. 247 vo.
" " 34, fol. 5.

In his report to the King on this subject the Conde de Linhares observed that there was no fear of the fidelity of the English in respect of this chartered vessel, nor that the Dutch would break with the English by capturing it; but he remarked that it would not be desirable to extend the practice of freighting foreign vessels. At the same time very strict orders were sent to the Government of Macao with regard to this ship, especially with the view of preventing the English from having direct intercourse with the Chinese.

D. R., Livro 34, fol. 41, 63 vo. and 66.

In a letter of 30th November 1635 to the King, the Viceroy strongly impressed upon His Majesty the importance of providing him with a sufficient force to defeat the

D. R., Livro 34, fol. 39.

* This voyage is referred to in further detail in the section "China." The ship chartered to the Portuguese was the "London"; this transaction is referred to in the "Surat Consultations" of 28th March 1635.

Dutch, in which event, he said, they would be discredited and refused trade in these parts, since they were everywhere cordially hated, and only succeeded in carrying on trade by means of the forces at their command.

D. R., Livro 37, fol. 481.

In consequence of the treaty above referred to, the English* were allowed to hire a house in Goa, and to establish trade there on payment of the customary duties. Accordingly five vessels arrived there in October 1636, and remained until the 8th February in the following year. Thence they went to Surat, and afterwards to Kanara, where they offered to purchase pepper at a higher price than the Portuguese were in the habit of paying. On this becoming known, the latter were very indignant. Some English ships about this time went to Baticala,† whence an Ambassador was despatched to Verabadanique‡ with offers to purchase pepper, after which the Portuguese noticed a coolness on the part of Verabadanique towards them, which they not unnaturally attributed to the actions of the English.

D. R., Livro 38, fol. 291.

D. R., Livro 40, fol. 116.

Shortly after this the Viceroy addressed a long letter to the King, dated 5th October 1637, wherein he remarked

---

* The record contained in this and the following paragraph, so far as it refers to the proceedings of the English, relates to Captain Weddel of "Courten's Association," and not to the East India Company. Evidently the Portuguese Viceroy did not distinguish between the two. From another document it appears that Captain Weddel and Nathaniel Mounteney, factor, took out a necklace and medallion as a present to the Portuguese Viceroy (Livro 38, fol. 285).

† Bhatkal. A town in the Honavar sub-division, North Kanara District. This was once a flourishing centre of trade, where merchants from Ormuz and Goa came to load sugar and rice.—*Imperial Gazetteer*.

‡ This is probably intended for Venkatappa Naik, an independent Chieftain of Bednur, and Ruler of Honavar.

that the bad return made by the English* for the friendship of the Portuguese was increasing. Not only did they take pepper from the lands of Kanara, which the Portuguese claimed as theirs, but they had endeavoured to turn Verabadanique and other kings against them. The English, he said, had associated themselves with a pirate named Babia, and they had established a factory at Baticala, within the jurisdiction of Verabadanique, for the purpose of collecting pepper, for which they exchanged copper and lead, giving higher prices than the Portuguese, and they had also made him presents, including a piece of artillery. All this proved, in the Viceroy's opinion, that the English were not a people with whom the Portuguese could have any commercial transactions, but he did not think it would be advisable to give up the armistice in consequence of this. Orders had, however, been given to all the Portuguese fortresses to have no trade with the English, but so to manage this as to avoid any rupture with them. If their ships were driven by stress of weather or otherwise into a Portuguese port, the Commandant was to help them in every possible way, but not to allow them to carry on commerce or to remain on shore any length of time. Special orders were given to the effect that on no account were any vessels, either large or small, to be sold to the English, although it would appear that promises had in former years been made that they might buy ships of the Portuguese; and, in order to prevent them from taking this in bad part, the excuse was to be made that, in future, vessels were only to be sold to Portuguese purchasers. News had been received at Goa that the

* In a subsequent letter of December 1637 the Viceroy remarked that the armistice continued with the English, but they were not allowed to trade with the Portuguese factories, as they endeavoured to take away their trade, and set them on unfriendly terms with neighbouring kings (D. R., Livro 40, fol. 209).

English were endeavouring to establish a factory at a port called Covalãs, situated two leagues to the south of the city of St. Thomé, for which purpose they had obtained permission from the lord of the land; orders were accordingly issued to the Captain General of Meliapore that he was to use every possible means to prevent this, to which end also the Viceroy despatched an ambassador to Verabadanique.

In consequence of robberies from three Portuguese vessels at Diu, said to have been perpetrated by an English pirate, the Viceroy sent out a vessel of war to capture him. As the President at Surat refused to give any satisfaction, orders were given that the property of the English in Goa should be seized, and the matter was handed over to the Tribunal of the Second Instance in Goa. It appears that a proposal had been made by the English President that the Portuguese should for the future carry on their trade in English vessels, but the Viceroy pointed out in a letter home that such a course as this would involve both a loss of reputation and a distinct disadvantage; besides, he remarked, it was evident that the sole object of the English in making this proposal was that they might get the entire trade into their own hands.

D. R., Livro 40, fol. 321.

In a letter of the 25th July 1637, Mr. Methwold, the English President, writing to the Viceroy, entirely repudiated the action of Captain Weddel, which, he remarked, had brought great disgrace upon the English name, and loss and discredit to the English East India Company. Mr. Methwold bore willing testimony to the fact that when English vessels put into Portuguese ports they were always well received, and stated that he invariably endeavoured to reciprocate that treatment. He also informed the Viceroy that he had declined offers of pepper at Cananore in order to avoid giving offence to the Portuguese; and he added that he had always kept one eye on the desire of being friendly towards the Portuguese, and the other to serve the interest of his employers.

When Portugal threw off the Spanish yoke, a Treaty of Peace and Commerce was concluded between King Charles I. and Dom João IV., King of Portugal, dated 29th January 1642, the twelfth clause* of which dealt specially with the Indian trade. In a letter referring to this Treaty, dated 30th December 1643, the Viceroy remarked that he was keeping on good terms with the English because the way in which they behaved merited it; he was also on good terms with the Danes, whose Company was, however, he observed "in a miserable state."

D. R., Livro 48, fol. 114.

The successful competition of the English with the Portuguese in trade must have been severely felt by them, since the King sent out orders in March 1643 that every effort should be made to prevent the English from getting pepper. Great care was, however, to be taken in this matter not to offend them, as they were so strong. In his reply the Viceroy remarked that he had always enjoyed friendly association with the English; and in a letter to the Portuguese Ambassador in London, of 18th November 1643, he said that the armistice arranged with the English had been carried out with

D. R., Livro 48, fol. 191.

D. R., Livro 48, fol. 285.

* XII. "And that the Treaty of Truce made between Don Michael de Noronha, Conde de Linhares, Viceroy of Goa, and William Methwold, President of the English in the East Indies, the 20th of January 1635, N.S., shall be continued and kept between the subjects of both Kings in the East Indies, and in all the States of the most renowned King of Portugal beyond the Cape of Good Hope; and that the Commissioners to be named by both Kings shall within three months take cognizance of the demands which have been or shall be made by the subjects and ships of the said Kings in the East Indies, with relation to their commerce in the said Indies; that so, by this means, a perpetual peace and alliance may be established and confirmed by both Kings between their subjects on both sides."—(F. O. Library, 4to., No. 3698, p. 327.)

the greatest punctuality, "very different from the "Dutch." But, notwithstanding the friendly relations now existing between the two countries, the King of Portugal sent out an order the following year that the English at Cochin should not be allowed to buy cinnamon, or drugs of any kind, and that every effort was to be made to prevent them from trading at Kanara. To this the Viceroy replied that the best way to effect that object would be to supply him with money to enable him to buy up all the pepper; the King, however, had to admit his inability to carry out that proposal, owing to the want of means and the great rise in the value of silver. In this same year, however, the Camara of Goa complained to the King that, owing to the want of vessels, the English had been taking cinnamon and other drugs instead of these going in Portuguese bottoms; to which His Majesty replied that the good understanding with the English was not meant to be extended to allowing them to export those articles to the detriment of the Royal finances.

D. R., Livro 48, fol. 309 vo.

D. R., Livro 55, fol. 31.

D. R., Livro 54, fol. 69.

We must now go back in point of date, in order to follow some of the principal events detailed in the Portuguese Records, relating to their proceedings with the Dutch in India during the half century to which I have limited this section.

The Dutch very soon obtained a dangerous predominance of trade, and in a letter of 1623 the King impressed upon the Viceroy the necessity of traversing their commerce, since it was most important, in the Royal interests, to put a stop, as early as possible, to the efforts of the English, Dutch, and French to take part in, and appropriate, the commerce of the East Indies, China, and Persia. Considering that it was practically impossible to turn out the English and Dutch by force of arms, because their strength in the

Eastern seas was great, and the Royal Treasury was exhausted, it was pointed out that cunning and diligence must be employed in order to destroy their trade, which, it was stated, was the real source of their strength. To this end it was proposed to allow pepper and cinnamon, which were then prohibited in Persia, to be taken there, forming a Company of careful merchants in imitation of the Dutch, and coming to an agreement with the Shah for an exchange of spices for silk, reasonable prices being fixed for all articles, so that the combination might be lasting. Spices, &c., would go thence to Moscovia and Turkey, and be spread over those northern countries which Holland then supplied through Port S. Nicholas and the Levant. The commerce of the Dutch would thus be destroyed, or they would have to compete against lower prices. Nothing, however, came of this very ingenious scheme.

The Dutch, who at first confined their trade to Java and the more eastern islands, were not long before they turned their attention to the Portuguese possessions in India. Their first point of attack appears to have been Meliapore,* which place they blockaded and took all vessels going thence. In a letter of 24th February 1635 it is remarked that this, once the wealthiest city in India, was now reduced both in population and commerce. In a letter, without date, but supposed to be about the year 1635, we find an account of a Dutch fleet of two ships having met a Portuguese fleet in the north, when it appears the latter got into disorder, owing to the wind being in favour of the enemy, and two of their vessels were captured. In the following year the Viceroy lamented that trade had fallen into the hands of the Dutch; that whereas India might have been

D. R., Livro 33, fol. 53.

D. R., Livro 33, fol. 263.

* S. Thomé de Meliapor, founded by the Portuguese in 1504; now a suburb of Madras.

the richest jewel in the Portuguese crown, all her forts were in a state of decay. About this time the King of Bisnaga offered to hand over to the Portuguese, or to pull down, the fortress at Trevanapatam, which had been built by the Malay King to give to the Dutch; on this, however, the King of Spain remarked that preference should, above all others things, be given to turning the Dutch out of the coast of Coromandel.

D. R., Livro 36, fol. 43.

In January 1637 a Dutch fleet of ten vessels appeared before the bar of Goa, with the intention of preventing the Portuguese vessels from going out on their homeward voyage. The Viceroy accordingly sent out a fleet on the 26th of that month to engage them, which obtained a great victory; and a second equally successful engagement is reported to have taken place on the 11th February, when twenty-four Portuguese vessels attacked the enemy. But notwithstanding these victories the ten Dutch vessels still retained their position off Goa, and they despatched an embassy to Adil Shah, asking his assistance to drive the Portuguese out of Goa, at the same time requesting for themselves permission to establish a fortress at Vingorla; this embassy was well received, and Adil Shah granted a firman for the establishment of a Dutch factory at Vingorla, where accordingly three of their company remained. This permission, however, he appears to have withdrawn shortly afterwards. They also sent another ambassador to the Mogul with very similar proposals for assistance against the Portuguese.

D. R., Livro 37, fols. 503 and 505.

D. R., Livro 40, fol. 134.

D. R., Livro 41, fol. 60 vo.

The Dutch fleet remained off Goa till the end of April, having been there for three months; during which time, however, it is claimed that they did not capture a single Portuguese ship, but only one belonging to a

D. R., Livro 40, fol. 134.

Moor of Portugal. On the 26th of the following October (1637) sixteen Dutch vessels of various sizes, under Admiral Adamus Werter Vuolt, again appeared off the bar of Goa, and the Portuguese, thinking they intended to attack the place, made every preparation to receive them, but they left again on the 26th November, sailing northwards, and went to Bassein, where they endeavoured to move a vessel that was being built there. The Dutch appear to have returned again to Goa shortly afterwards, for I find that on the 4th January 1638 the Viceroy sent out a fleet to attack them off that port. The fight commenced at 8 a.m., and after a severe conflict the enemy were driven off with the loss of two of their vessels, whilst the Portuguese lost one of theirs. On the 15th April following a Treaty was concluded by Admiral Vuolt with the Reverend Frey Fernando de Lahore, in which it was agreed that in the event of Generals being taken prisoners they should be exchanged equally, viz., General for General, and in the event of the number not being equal, the price of ransom should be 200 patacas for each General. Admirals taken prisoners were to be exchanged in like manner, with a ransom of 150 patacas for each Admiral in excess. Captains were to be ransomed at 100 patacas. All women captured, whether Portuguese or Dutch, to be given up respectively without the payment of any ransom. Members of a religious order, not being either Bishop, Archbishop, or Patriarch, to be ransomed at the rate of 40 patacas each. All other prisoners, when practicable, were to be exchanged prisoner for prisoner, or ransomed at the rate of 10 patacas each. In this year also a Dutch fleet of seven vessels came upon a Portuguese fleet at anchor off

D. R., Livro 40, fol. 160.

D. R., Livro 40, fol. 4.

D. R., Livro 40, fol. 235.

Tratados, T. II., fol. 86.

D. R., Livro 41, fol. 12.

Puludindin, which they attacked so vigorously that they destroyed them all, and only the crews of half of them escaped to land.

In writing to the King about the Dutch in India, under date 31st August 1638, the Viceroy remarked that they had a monopoly of trade in China, from the Bay of Cochin China down to the point of Sunda. In Cochin China and Tonquin they had established large factories, and had also opened up commerce on the Amoy river, immediately opposite the Island of Formosa, where they exchanged pepper for silk, and whence also they traded to Japan. They had, too, started factories at Camboja, Siam, Borneo, Amboyna, Maluco, Jamby, and Dandarquim, besides enjoying the lordship of the islands of Banda, and of many other places, as far as Achin. In the Bay of Bengal they had ample commerce at the ports on the coast of Gergelim, Masulipatam, Paliacate, Trevanapatam, and other factories above Galle, as well as in the kingdoms of Bisnaga, Golconda, and in the provinces of the Mogul and of Adil Shah, besides enormous commerce with Surat, Persia, the Straits of Mecca, and many islands in the Eastern seas. The King expressed great concern at the state of affairs in India, but explained that it was impossible for him to send out any more vessels, as he had recently despatched a large fleet to the Brazils to dislodge the enemy there. In a letter of 1st March 1639 the Viceroy declared it to be impossible to carry on in India any longer without relief, and that if no succour could be sent it would only remain to wind up the affairs of the State in the East and to retire.

D. R., Livro 41, fol. 16.

D. R., Livro 44, fol. 194.

D. R., Livro 44, fol. 249.

On the 15th November 1638 a fleet of eleven Dutch vessels appeared before Goa, and blockaded the port, at the same time sending an am-

D. R., Livro 44, fols. 250 and 251.

bassador to Adil Shah, proposing that he should join them in driving out the Portuguese, who, being unable to get their vessels out of the port, also sent an ambassador to Adil Shah with the view of obtaining his assistance against the Dutch. The latter were, however, allowed to retain their Factory at Vingorla, and they were further negotiating for another one at Karwar, where the English were also endeavouring to obtain a site for a similar purpose. In January 1639 a Portuguese fleet arrived from the Cape, and other vessels from Coromandel, which succeeded in entering the harbour. A Council was then held to consider the advisability of fighting the enemy, which the Viceroy was anxious to do, but he was overruled by his Council, who considered that it would be more to the advantage of the State to send a strong fleet to the relief of Ceylon. In February, the Dutch fleet left Goa and went to Ceylon to the assistance of the King of Candia. The Portuguese trade with the South was now reduced to being carried on in rowing vessels, which could more easily escape the enemy's ships. The Naique of Maduré sent his ambassador, Ramapa, to the Viceroy, on the 13th August 1639, to give an assurance on his account to the King of Portugal that, in consideration of the assistance sent him when he wished to take Marava,* he undertook to give the King of Portugal a fortress in Pampa, called Uthear, or wherever he might desire one, with a Portuguese Captain, 50 Portuguese soldiers, 100 lascars, and 3,000 pardaos, for the maintenance of the same; also to build at his own expense a church at Ramanacor,† and seven churches between Bambam and Tomddy.‡ The Naique also gave permission to all those who might desire it to become

Tratados, T. II., p. 103.

* Marava was probably a name given to the sea coast of the Ramnad Zamindari, since, according to the Gazetteer of Madura, the Maravans were a caste inhabiting that district.

† Ramnad.

‡ Between Pambam and Tondi.

Christians, and promised to furnish gratuitously to the King of Portugal all the assistance he might require for Ceylon, both in men and supplies. He further undertook not to be friendly to the Dutch, nor to permit them in his territories, whilst his vassals would also not be permitted to visit Dutch ports.

Tratados, T. II., p. 108.

As soon as Portugal recovered her independence a treaty of peace was concluded, on the 12th June 1641, between King Dom João IV. and the United Provinces of the Netherlands, in which it was stipulated as follows:—In the East Indies, and in all the lands and seas under the jurisdiction granted by the States General to the East India Company, this treaty was to come into force one year after the date of its signature. Should, however, the proclamation of peace reach any of those lands before that year had expired, all acts of hostility were to cease at once. All the Kings, Sovereigns, and nations in the East Indies who might be friends of, or in confederation with, the States General, or the East India Company of the United Provinces, were to be included in this treaty. All Portuguese ships from Portugal to those parts and *vice versâ* were not to be molested, and to have perfect freedom on the seas for the space of ten years; and in the same way the ships of the United Provinces were not to be molested either. The subjects of the East India Company of the United Provinces were to enjoy, in the dominions of the King of Portugal, the same exemptions and liberties and rights as the other subjects of the United Provinces enjoyed under this treaty, provided the East India Company and its subjects did not convey from Brazil, sugar, Brazilian wood, or any other Brazilian product to Portugal, and the Portuguese did not convey the same from Brazil to the said Provinces. The Dutch and Portuguese were to aid each other, should occasion arise, while this treaty lasted. Every subject of one or the other part should be left as he was, and in possession of his goods as he should be possessed of the same at the time this treaty was proclaimed, and all the lands and districts between the forts of one and the other should remain as they were.

Before the actual signing of this treaty King Dom João IV., in announcing his accession to the throne of Portugal, stated (18th March 1641) that he had received offers both from the English and Dutch to assist him. With regard to the Dutch he instructed the Viceroy to inform them that all causes for war had now ceased, an armistice was to be declared and no hostilities were to be commenced pending further orders. The Native Princes in India were also to be informed that there would be now no further wars between the Europeans in India.

D. R., Livro 48, fol. 53.

The hopes that dictated this letter were, however, not destined to be realized. On 16th October following, a Dutch fleet, consisting of four large and two small vessels, arrived off Goa, and these were a few days after joined temporarily by two more large ships. Some months later a Portuguese fleet, sailing towards India, met with a Dutch fleet, whereupon an engagement ensued, in which the latter was defeated. In India the Dutch still continued to molest the Portuguese, and declined to desist until they should receive definite instructions from the Prince of Orange.

D. R., Livro 47, fol. 22.

D. R., Livro 48, fol. 114.

In a letter of 10th December 1643 it is stated that the Dutch had then been blockading Goa for six years, in consequence of which the Viceroy sent two ambassadors to Batavia on board a Dutch ship, as the only available means of relieving the port of their presence. These, however, returned with the information that the ratification of the treaty had not yet reached Batavia, and the Dutch Governor accordingly ordered his vessels to continue the blockade. Eight days later the Viceroy

D. R., Livro 48, fol. 115.

reported that a Portuguese fleet going to the relief of St. Thomé had met with a Dutch fleet off Negapatam. This fleet had arrived there on the 12th April, summoned the place to surrender, and landed 600 men who had taken possession of it; the inhabitants, however, paid a ransom for them to retire, and two days later the Portuguese fleet hove in sight, whereupon the Dutch troops re-embarked with all speed. An engagement ensued, in which the Portuguese lost two ships, but otherwise the action seems to have been indecisive, except that the Dutch fleet retired; the Viceroy, however, claimed that the action had relieved Negapatam and Ceylon.

D. R., Livro 48, fols. 118 vo., 119 vo.

As an illustration of the manner in which the Dutch conducted themselves towards the Portuguese, the Viceroy reported, in December 1643, that two merchant vessels, sailing from Muscat for Chaul, were met by five Dutch ships proceeding from Goa to Surat, which, upon sighting them, hoisted a white flag. One of the Portuguese vessels, falling into the trap, did not change its course, and was boarded and captured by the Dutch; the other, fearing possible consequences, had steered clear of the enemy and escaped. The Viceroy had appealed to the Dutch Commodore at Surat against this breach of the armistice, although he entertained but little hope of his claim being attended to.

D. R., Livro 48, fol. 142.

It appears that the armistice was published in Batavia in November 1642 and in Malacca on 5th December, whereupon news was sent home to the States that the armistice had been carried out. On the 5th March 1645, however, it had not been published in Goa, owing to delays on the part of the Dutch, which the Viceroy attributed to a desire on their part to prevent, if possible, any Portuguese vessels leaving at the proper season for home. On the 2nd

D. R., Livro 48, fols. 149, 151, 187, 268.

March, however, the Dutch Commissioner had indeed arrived in India with the armistice, but he proceeded first to Galle,* where he declined to publish it. He then proceeded to Goa, where he arrived on the 1st April, and here also he declined to publish the armistice unless the Portuguese would first give up the lands round Galle, which they declined to do; whereupon Pedro Boreel, the Dutch Commissioner, returned on board his vessel on the 23rd, declaring that the war between the two nations in India should continue on the same footing as heretofore, against which the Viceroy solemnly protested. In September following fourteen Dutch vessels again appeared off the bar of Goa, and as the Viceroy still declined to accede to the demands with regard to the lands at Galle, the blockade was renewed, and the Portuguese vessels, which had now been shut up in that harbour for four years, were unable to go home. The Dutch commander had, however, it appears, no instructions authorizing him to take any warlike measures against the place. About this time the Viceroy reported that Adil Shah had offered, for a certain sum of money, to turn the Dutch out of his territory and never more admit them, and he advocated, at the time, the adoption of this course. Owing, however, to the change of Government in Portugal, and the hopes still entertained of coming to an agreement with respect to the armistice, no further steps were taken in the matter.

D. R., Livro 51, fol. 23.

In 1645 the English and Dutch had both succeeded in carrying on trade in Goa, and they obtained cinnamon there, some of which was, it was alleged, the property of the Portuguese State. The Moors, it would seem, declined to take precious stones or other merchandise into Goa on account of the duties there, but sold them to the English and Dutch either

D. R., Livro 56, fols. 125, 138.

* For further details, *see* section on "Ceylon."

from their ships direct on the bar of Goa, or at ports where there were no duties. Similarly, private individuals amongst the Portuguese on the Coromandel coast carried on commerce with the English and Dutch, avoiding the duties at the Portuguese ports.

D. R., Livro 51, fol. 386 vo.

The King sent out orders in cipher in February 1646, that the Native Kings should be induced to fight against the Dutch. The Viceroy in reply stated that the Dutch were already doing the Portuguese as much harm as they could in spite of the armistice, and that he had despatched envoys to the several native Kings for the purpose suggested. The Materan replied that if an opportunity offered he would be very glad to fight the Dutch; the King of Bantam had made peace with the Dutch for so long as the latter remained on terms of peace with the Portuguese. The King of Macassar was on good terms with the Portuguese, and although he was at peace and had transactions with the Dutch, this was more through fear than desire. The King of Camboja had turned the Dutch out. The Chincheu* had also turned them out; from him they used to get silk for Japan, but they could no longer draw it from there, and they were keeping up their trade in Japan with leather and other goods they got from Siam. An ambassador had been sent to Achin and Johore, the latter of whom was carrying on war with Malacca, and so injuring the Dutch trade there. The King of Candia had fallen out with the Dutch, and taken and beheaded more than five hundred of their men.

D. R., Livro 59, fol. 50, 51.

It appears that in 1648 the Naik turned the Dutch out of Pattanam, where they had established a Factory, and the Captain-General on leaving the place threatened the Portuguese that they would eventually have to settle with him for this matter. Accordingly, on the

* Chinchew; a port of Fuhkien, in China.

7th February 1649, there appeared off Manapad a fleet of ten Dutch vessels, under the command of J. M. Suycher, Governor of Galle. Two days afterwards they arrived off Pattanam,* and disembarked some Dutch and Cingalese infantry near the Pagoda of Trickendur, which they took, with the cattle it contained, and fortified and armed it with artillery. As soon as the inhabitants of Tuticorin were informed of the arrival of the Dutch, they sent messengers to protest, in the name of the King of Portugal, against their proceedings; these, however, were received by the Dutch commander with contempt and threats of hostilities. On the 12th the Dutch marched upon the town, which they entered without resistance,† and disarmed all the Portuguese they met with. The Dutch then stated it was well known that their factor had been turned out of Pattanam by the intrigues of the Paravas‡ with the Native King, but that they would limit their revenge to laying a forced contribution of 40,000 patacas,§ and if it were not paid immediately they threatened to build a fortress in Tuticorin so as to enable them to hold the town and dominate the remainder of the coast. The money not being forthcoming at the end of three days they sacked the town and burnt a part of it. They then reduced their demand to 20,000 patacas, and subsequently to 15,000; but being unable to force this latter amount from the people they finally contented themselves with removing everything of value they could lay hands on, and they then compelled the Portuguese monks to sign a paper binding themselves to make the Paravas pay the money; having done this they again fired the place and went on board their vessels, taking

D. R., Livro 58, fol. 66.

* Probably Caylpatnam, between Tuticorin and Manapad, where there was once a Dutch factory.

† There is no account of this capture of Tuticorin by the Dutch in any of our histories.

‡ Inhabitants of the fishing coast.

§ A term formerly much in use for a dollar, or piece of eight.

nearly all the fishing boats belonging to the inhabitants for the conveyance of the spoil. They then left on the 13th February.

I have already referred to the communications had by the Portuguese with the native powers to assist them against the Dutch, but must now give an account of their relations with them in somewhat fuller detail.

The King of Bisnaga* had made over the territories of Bardez and Salsette to the Portuguese in 1521. By a Treaty of the 26th February 1546 he swore eternal friendship to the King of Portugal; confirmed the deed of gift of the territories of Bardez and Salsette, and swore that he would never make war against those provinces. By a Treaty concluded with the King of Bisnaga on the 19th September 1547, the Viceroy allowed him to take from the City of Goa all the horses which might arrive there for him from Persia and Arabia, but bound himself not to allow any to be sent to the Adil Shah. At the same time the King of Bisnaga agreed not to allow any provisions or supplies to be sent from his territories, or from the kingdom of Benguapor to the territories of the Adil Shah.

Tratados, T. I., p. 116.

Tratados, T. I., p. 118.

On the 6th October 1547 the Governor, Dom João de Castro entered into an agreement with King Iniza Moxá,† in which they mutually swore friendship and undertook to help each other, when necessary, against all the kings in India with the exception of the King of Bisnaga. The Governor further bound himself not to make peace with the Adil Shah without previously giving

Tratados, T. I., p. 120.

* In 1521 the King of Bisnaga, who had captured all the territories of the Adil Shah, made a free gift of them to the King of Portugal, and the Viceroy took possession of them accordingly. *Lendas da India*, Vol. II., Pt. II., p. 658.

† This is the same person as Nizamaluco, Lord of Chaul.

notice to Iniza Moxá. D. João de Castro was succeeded as Governor by Garcia de Sá, and he, on the 22nd August 1548, concluded a treaty with the Adil Shah under which the latter undertook to release all captives, and renewed the agreement that the territories of Salsette and Bardez should be the property of the King of Portugal for ever. Should the Rumes send a fleet against the Portuguese, he undertook to help the latter with men and supplies.

Tratados, T. I., p. 122.

On the 17th September following, Garcia de Sá concluded a contract with the Queen of Baticalá, under which she undertook to pay the annual tribute previously promised to the King of Portugal, as well as all arrears due on account of past years. She also promised not to permit any pirate fleets to leave her territories, and in the event of her failure to restrain them she made herself personally responsible for any damage the Portuguese might suffer in consequence.

Tratados, T. I., p. 130.

By a Treaty of the 17th December 1571 the Adil Shah agreed that should any enemies attack the Portuguese either by land or sea he would assist in driving them away. And by a subsequent Treaty of the 30th May 1575 it was stipulated that before the Adil Shah made war against anybody he should give notice to the Governor of India in order that the latter might look into the cause of hostilities, and, in the event of its appearing reasonable, make preparations for assisting him.

Tratados, T. I., p. 161.

Tratados, T. I., p. 167.

Through the intervention of the Adil Shah, a Treaty was concluded, on the 9th October 1615, with Iniźa Moxá, in accordance with which the latter agreed not to give shelter to, or allow the entry into his ports and territories by, the British or Dutch, nor in other ways extend any favour to them.

Tratados, T. I., p. 192.

The King of Asarceta* concluded a treaty of peace with the Captain of Daman, dated the 12th March 1635, by which he agreed that neither he nor his Captains should ever assist any enemy of the Portuguese; that he would send assistance to the Captains and Governors of Daman in time of war when called upon to do so; and that in the event of his wishing to declare war against an enemy he would first give notice to the Captain, in order that he might investigate the justice of the case and make preparations to assist the king.

Tratados, T. II., p. 61.

About the same time (1635) an arrangement was entered into between the Viceroy and the Raja of Bisnaga by which the latter was to assist in turning the Dutch out of Paliacate. The Raja's forces were to attack the place by land and the Portuguese by sea. When it was taken the Raja was to receive 30,000 xerafins, 12 horses, and 6 elephants as his share of the spoil. On the good success of this undertaking, the King of Portugal remarked, depended the depriving the Dutch of the trade in cloths on the coast of Coromandel, and of the commerce of the south. A fleet of 12 vessels was accordingly sent by the Portuguese, but Bisnaga failed to carry out his engagement; this, he afterwards explained, was due to a disturbance in his own dominions, but that having put this down he was prepared to fulfil his obligations. The Portuguese fleet had, however, now left Paliacate, whence it proceeded to Tuticorin to punish the Naique of Madura, and to overawe the Jesuits there; the former having seized, at the instance of the latter, a

D. R., Livro 32, fol. 9.

D. R., Livro 33, fols. 9 and 253.

D. R., Livro 34, fol. 15.

* Elsewhere spelt Sarceta. According to Bocarro this place was situated five leagues to the north of Daman.

Portuguese agent who had been sent to purchase saltpetre in exchange for elephants. A second expedition was sent by the Portuguese against Paliacate, but again the King of Bisnaga failed to take part in it, and the Viceroy accordingly expressed an opinion that he was not to be relied on. Subsequently, however, the Raja did attack Paliacate, but coming to terms with the enemy he raised the siege, leaving the Dutch in uninterrupted possession, in consideration of which it was reported that he received from them 20,000 pardaos.

D. R., Livro 37, fol. 15.

When Shah Jehan invaded the Deccan in 1635, the King of Spain gave orders that the Adil Shah and the Melique were to be assisted against him in order, if possible, to check his growing power. It was reported that the Mogul had left Agra with 60,000 horsemen to make war upon the Adil Shah, and he sent an Ambassador in advance, demanding the surrender of the whole of the Melique's kingdom, and the payment of 30 million pagodas of arrears. The Melique is said to have been surrounded by councillors who were in the interest of the Mogul, and it was feared by the Portuguese that if the latter succeeded in getting possession of Melique and Kanara, he would next descend upon their territory. The Viceroy, in a letter to the King of the 30th December 1635, expressed a fear that the Adil Shah would lose his kingdom to the Mogul, in which case the Portuguese possessions would be in great danger. The Adil Shah appears to have been in a great strait, for in a letter from the King to the Viceroy of the 28th January 1636 it is stated that whilst he was, on the one hand, negotiating terms with the Portuguese, he also threatened to propose

D. R., Livro 32, fol. 15.
" " 33, fol. 15.

D. R., Livro 33, fol. 258.

D. R., Livro 34, fol. 39.

D. R., Livro 36, fol. 61.

terms to the English and Dutch to turn them out of Goa. The Viceroy reported

D. R., Livro 36, fol. 149.

that the Mogul had made overtures to the Portuguese to assist him against the Adil Shah, which he had refused; but his successor, the Conde de Linhares, denied

D. R., Livro 37, fol. 21.

this, and stated that the proposal emanated from the English and Dutch. Shortly afterwards the Dutch sent an Ambassador to the Adil Shah asking his assistance to drive the Portuguese out of Goa, and requesting

D. R., Livro 37, fol. 505.

permission to establish a fortress at Vingorla; they also sent another Ambassador to the Mogul making somewhat similar proposals. The Adil Shah was at last conquered by the Mogul and reduced by him to the

D. R., Livro 40, fol. 10.

position of a Thanadar, by whom he was also prohibited from using an umbrella and from calling himself Adil Shah, as he was now a vassal. It appears that no assistance was rendered to him by the Portuguese, on the plea that he had not asked for it. The Mogul

D. R., Livro 40, fol. 130.

placed the Adil Shah's territory in charge of his son Aurangzeb, who showed himself favourable to the Portuguese. In reporting this to the King, the Viceroy remarked,

Tratados, T. II., fol. 100.

in a letter of 11th September 1638, that of all the Eastern kingdoms between the Indus and the Ganges, that of the Mogul was the most prosperous. He had brought to his empire all the kingdoms of Bengal, and made tributaries the kinglets of the coast of Gergetim as far as Masulipatam; he had also recently acquired the great kingdom of Decany. In the year 1632 he had sent a great army to Visapor, belonging to the Adil Shah, which he had also made tributary to himself. The Mogul had, too, he reported, demanded and obtained tribute from the territories of Colle. It is clear, however, that the Adil Shah still retained very considerable power and authority, for I find that, about the year 1639, the Viceroy had, by his Ambassadors, induced him to turn the English (Courten's Association) out of Baticalá and to level their factory there.

D. R., Livro 44, fol. 253 vo.

Writing in December 1643 the Viceroy reported that the Zamorin and the Adil Shah, as well as the Princes of Malabar, were all on good terms with the Portuguese. In the following year the King of Quilon offered the Portuguese a site for the erection of a fort at Olala* in his kingdom, which, however, they were unable to accept owing to the want of means either to build or maintain it. In 1646 the King of the Maldive Islands signed a treaty of vassalage to the King of Portugal. No copy of this treaty appears to have been preserved; but there exists a letter from the King of the Maldives, dated 5th May 1643, in which it is stated that under an agreement of former years he was bound to deliver to the Viceroy one-third of the coir fibre which he received as tribute.

D. R., Livro 48, fol. 127.

D. R., Livro 55, fol. 1.

D. R., Livro 55, fol. 96.

D. R., Livro 54, fol. 139.

Towards the end of the period to which the present section of my report refers the Genoese appear to have made an attempt to recover a portion at least of the Indo-European trade, of whose expedition the following account is given in the Portuguese records.

In the year 1648 some private Genoese and other merchants, under Letters Patent from the Duke and Senate of that city, equipped two large ships, the "St. John the Baptist" and the "St. Bernard," for the purpose, as they gave out, of discovering new lands un-

D. R., Livro 58, fol. 55.

---

* On the coast of Kanara, near Mangalore.

inhabited, or unexplored by European commerce, and also to take advantage of the Eastern commerce in a way not offensive to the other nations engaged therein. This enterprise was started at the instance of William Mulman, of Amsterdam, whose brother Henry Mulman was then Dutch Consul at Genoa. The Company consisted of thirty persons, some of whom were Genoese and the rest foreigners. Two men were sent from Amsterdam, one to act as Chief Pilot and the other as Chief Factor. The two vessels were bought at Amsterdam, and were built on the same lines as those of the Dutch East India Company. They went from that port equipped with provisions, arms, and artillery for three years, their cargoes consisting of knives, guns, gun-metal, and other articles useful for barter with the natives. The two Dutchmen above referred to were engaged on the terms of receiving one-fifth of the profits.

The ships sailed from Genoa on the 3rd March 1648; they put in at Alicante and Malaga, where they procured wine, and passing the Straits of Gibraltar they took in salt at Cape de Verde, and water and wood at Sierra Leone. At the port of Antongil, in the island of S. Laurenço (Madagascar) they stayed a month to recruit, and there the Chief Factor died on board the "St. Bernard," the Captain of which refused to obey the orders of the other Dutchman, who therefore prepared to reduce him to obedience by force of arms; some Genoese gentlemen on the other vessel, however, intervened and, going on board the "St. Bernard," persuaded the Captain of it to go on the "St. John" and disouss the matter. He did so, and was immeliately put in irons, his partisans also being severely punished. The vessels then continued their voyage in the direction of Goa, but were driven by stress of weather into the port of Ticos,* on the coast of Java.

* The nearest approach to this name seems to be Tegal, on the north coast of Java; but it was more probably Tiku, on the coast of Sumatra.

Here the Dutchman endeavoured to take in pepper to sell in China, and made an agreement with the Governor of the country for the supply of a cargo, but was hindered in the transaction by the Malays, who accused him of being English and of carrying false money. The Dutchman settled the matter by taking the pepper without paying for it. The vessels then put into Felida to repair, where they stayed a month, and so gave an opportunity for the Malays they had robbed to complain to the Dutch General at Batavia, who immediately sent out eight vessels which captured the Genoese ships in the Straits of Sunda, and took them to Batavia. All Dutch subjects on board were taken ashore and imprisoned, whilst the Genoese were forced to sell their merchandise, and their vessels which they could no longer navigate.

PORTUGUESE INDIA.

Section III. 1650—1700.

During the first half of the seventeenth century the Portuguese had been engaged in incessant wars with the Dutch in India, and had at the same time to protect their interests in the Brazils against these and other rivals. Almost immediately after Portugal had passed under the Crown of Spain, English adventurers organized expeditions against the Brazils, and these were followed, in 1612, by the French. In 1624 the Dutch East India Company despatched a fleet against Bahia, and from that date they waged continual war against the Portuguese in the Brazils up to 1654, when, after a series of sanguinary encounters, the latter succeeded in re-establishing their supremacy in those parts.

They were not, however, so successful in the East. Ormuz had been lost to the combined Persian and English forces in 1622, and the other Portuguese possessions in the Persian Gulf fell successively to other opponents until Muscat, their last stronghold in those parts, was wrested from them by the Arabs in 1650. Their power in the further East was crippled by the loss of Malacca to the Dutch in 1641; and at the commencement of the period to which the present Section relates, the Portuguese had lost nearly all their possessions in Ceylon. Colombo fell in 1656, and Jafanapatam, their last possession in that island, in 1658*.

During the preceding half century of incessant wars both in India and in the Brazils the small kingdom of Portugal had been drained of both men and money. Trade had necessarily languished considerably and

* *Vide* Sections "Red Sea and Persian Gulf," "Ceylon," and "Malacca" respectively.

become almost extinguished. Not being possessed of territories in the neighbourhood of their forts and factories to yield revenues sufficient for their necessities, other and special means had to be adopted in order to raise funds to meet the expenses of their wars and Government.

MSS.

The Portuguese Records of the early part of the seventeenth century contain, as already stated (*see* p. 26), numerous orders from home to the Governors abroad that the money provided for the purchase of spices was to be devoted exclusively to the purposes for which it was supplied; and these orders, taken in conjunction with the record of repeated instances of officers in India being heavily indebted to the State, would seem to indicate the existence of misappropriation of funds on an extensive scale, which must have been most embarrassing to the proper administration of the Government. In 1621 the one per cent. tax, which had been originally levied for ecclesiastical purposes, was appropriated for the service of the State; and shortly afterwards, during the viceroyalty of D. Francisco da Gama (1622 to 1627), a two per cent. consular duty was levied at certain ports with the view of raising a fund for the equipment of a fleet to turn the Dutch out of India. Letters of marque were also issued to private persons, authorizing them to equip vessels to prey upon the Dutch ships, as the Government had not the means to provide them in sufficient quantities. As an additional means of raising funds for carrying on the administration of the State in India, the most important appointments were now put up to auction and sold to the highest bidders; an additional one per cent. consulate was levied at various ports in order to provide artillery for the forts; and the profits of special voyages were also appropriated to the repair of the fortresses. The wealth of the convents in India had already been appropriated by the

Government and absorbed in the general expenses of the administration, and thus the commencement of the second half of the seventeenth century found the Portuguese Viceroys in very embarrassed circumstances.

D. R., Livro 61, fols. 312, 581, 582.

An important evidence of the decay of the Portuguese power in India referred to in these Records is the fact that, in 1651, the King of Golconda and the Nabob Mirzi Mula had ceased to ask them for passports for their vessels. One reason of their desire not to quarrel with the English, given about this time, was the fact that they were dependent on the President of Surat for obtaining ropes and tar for the equipment of their fleets, which, owing to the absence of money, they were obliged to pay for with cinnamon. Mangalor was now reported to be in a dangerous state, owing to the decay of its fortifications and to the fact that all the surrounding country was in the possession of the King of Kanara; all the Portuguese fortresses in Kanara were in a similar state, but, as none of them possessed any commerce, it was impossible to repair them.

D. R., Livro 56, fol. 480.

On the 14th June 1652 the Fort of Cambolin was attacked by Seva Panaique.* The siege was commenced on the 6th September, after Barcelor had surrendered to his arms, and he was then able to bring from thence reinforcements to the extent of 8,000 men and ten pieces of artillery. During the siege seventy Portuguese were killed, and on the 17th January 1653 the defenders withdrew in some vessels which had been sent to their relief, taking with them all they could carry and leaving the fortress entirely dismantled. On the 25th October, during the siege, however, a fleet had come to

* Shivappa Naik, a Bednur Chief, who between 1648 and 1670 added to his dominions the whole of South Kanara, and North Kanara up to the Gangavali river.

the relief of the place and had fought with the enemy, losing some vessels; thirty-five days afterwards came another Portuguese fleet, which, however, retired after doing some damage to the enemy, and two days before the fort surrendered a third fleet arrived. These circumstances appeared so peculiar that an inquiry was instituted into the matter, which only resulted in the conclusion that the fortress was not in a defensible state. On this point there was some difference of opinion, and one witness attributed the surrender to the action of the Captain of the last relief, expressing it as his opinion that the fortress could have been defended for some time longer. The Viceroy, in summing up the evidence, came to the conclusion that the fortress was not in a defensible state, and he added that most of the other Portuguese fortresses in India were in a similar condition. On the arrival of Dom Vasco Mascarenhas as Viceroy, in September 1652, the war with Kanara was still progressing, and Honor and Mangalor were invested by the enemy; Seva Panaique, however, had sent two of his Brahmins to Honor to negotiate for peace.

D. R., Livro 56, fol. 491.

In 1654 proposals passed between the English and Portuguese for a union of interests with a view of driving the Dutch out of India. Circumstances at the time prevented the carrying out of this project, but it having come to the knowledge of the Dutch they sent a fleet to await the arrival of the English ships from Persia, which they met and defeated off Sind.* In this year also the Adil Shah,

Evord. Cod., CV. 2–15, fol. 46.

* It appears from the India Office Records that some time in December 1653, the ships *Falcon* (26 guns), *Dove* (24), and *Welcome* (32) sailed from Diu, with orders from the President and Council of Surat to proceed to Gombroon to convoy back the *Endeavour*, then at that port, and also to take up lading at Scindy and Rajapore. They reached the "Gulf of Persia" in safety, and found there two Dutch ships, which they engaged during the night for some hours. The

after 87 years of peace with the Portuguese, marched an army against Bardez and Goa, 5,000 strong, which arrived

---

English sailors, however, had little stomach for the fight; and at daybreak, the English, though the superior force, bore away to Ormuz to join the *Endeavour*. Both fleets then anchored in Gombroon Roads, and remained there two days, after which the English left the Dutch riding there, and sailed away to Scindy. On reaching that port, however, they found there five of the enemy's vessels, which at once weighed and encountered them (29th January 1653–4, *see* O. C., 2524). The following is the description of the fight given in a letter from the President and Council at Surat to the Company, dated 28th March 1654 (O. C., 2376) :—

"The Dutch Admiral, with the first broadside of the *Welcome*, who had brought 21 pieces of ordnance on that side, was happily laid by the lee, and did no service all the fight after. The *Falcon* as unhappily run stemlings on board her the said Admiral, but was soon cleared of her again, when presently she fell foul of another Dutch ship that lay astern of the Admiral, and by that means lost her foremast. The *Falcon* was entered by the Dutch out of this ship, which was a laden ship, inferior to the *Falcon* both in ordnance and number of men. They were aboard each other above an hour. The Dutch cleared themselves of the *Falcon* not without considerable loss, and the *Falcon* being clear of her and all other ships, a strange fear possessed them that their ship was on fire, and therefore would needs yield her up to the enemy, and shift for themselves in their boats, which they did and would not be persuaded to the contrary; though some that they left aboard and abhorred so cowardly an action endeavoured by all means they could. Above 60 able men that had not received the least hurt in the world run away in their boats, one of which boats went to the Dutch Admiral, as she lay by the lee, and they would not take them in, so were forced to row to another ship; the other boat got aboard the *Welcome*, who how she had bestowed her time all this while of the *Falcon's* encounter we cannot learn, but only she kept to windward, and was unwilling to come and help the *Falcon* when the Dutch was on board him, lest in firing at the one he should hurt the other. Mr. Hargreave with the boatswain of the *Falcon*, and about 10 well and wounded, were left aboard the ship, whom those that got aboard the *Welcome* desired they might be fetched off; which Mr. Walterer was endeavouring to do, but his men would not suffer him to bear to leeward, or send a boat; but thought they had done enough in preserving themselves, and so bore away after the *Dove*, who had the discretion to keep herself out of harm's way after the first coming up with the Dutch ships, being once got out of shot, scarce came within reach of a gun again, but so well preserved herself that she had not a man slain or hurt. The *Welcome* lost one and no other hurt. The *Endeavour* did best of any of them, for she not going well by a wind was soon put to leeward of the Dutch, not having

there on the 12th August, on which day there was an eclipse of the sun. In the Residency of Tevy* he found a few Portuguese without either food or arms, who retired into the Church, but afterwards surrendered at discretion. In the small fortress at that place there were 25 soldiers who defended themselves with great valour. Every effort was made at Goa to send a force as soon as possible to stop the advance of the enemy; but it was only on the 14th that 300 men could be got together at Panjim, from whence they marched against the invaders, and, after a severe fight, forced them to retire. This small force was, however, too exhausted to follow up their advantage. Later on, in October, the Adil Shah invaded Salsette with 7,000 foot and 800 horsemen, taking Sarzora in spite of some resistance. On the 3rd October he surrounded Cutuly with his entire force, and after three days fighting it surrendered. News having reached the Adil Shah that the

---

any to second her, and was encountered by two of the second best ships the Dutch had, with whom she maintained the fight, till she had received so many shot under and between wind and water, that she was ready to sink before she surrendered, for the Dutch coming aboard her, before they could get anything out of her, or their own people again, she sunk down, and with her 10 English and 11 or 13 Dutch men, and all perished, but in this time they were got above a league to leeward of the rest of the ships, nor did those two ships engage any ship in the fight only the *Endeavour*. Nor came they up with the Admiral again till within night, who a little before had made sail again, and stood after them that were running away as fast as they could, which had not God taken away their hearts might in all probability have had the day of the Dutch, for they were also very glad they were rid of them, as we were credibly informed by some, that was on board them, and especially from Monsieur Tavernier, who in brief gives this relation. Never was fight worse managed on both sides, the Dutch were most of them drunk, and knew not what they did, the English I think were little better, if not worse; they would never else have lost such an opportunity (thus M. Tavernier)."

The *Welcome* and *Dove* reached Surat the 5th February 1653-4. Two days later, two of the Dutch ships came in, "and brought the "*Falcon* in triumph with them, and about 80 of our men prisoners to "our no little dishonour." (O. C., 2362.)

* Probably Tevim, in Bardez.

Portuguese General was collecting forces at Rachol, all his troops were ordered to return to Vizapore with their prisoners and spoil, and a peace was subsequently concluded between the Adil Shah and the Portuguese. On account of this invasion the Portuguese were forced to raise the siege of Honor.

Tratados, T. II., p. 232.

The treaty concluded with the Adil Shah was dated the 7th March 1655. On the 3rd December an Ambassador from the Adil Shah arrived at Goa and presented a letter to the Viceroy, accompanied with some robes of Royal orders and other valuable presents. The Adil Shah admitted that, without any cause, he had declared war against the Portuguese, thus impeding trade and closing ports; that his captain had entered the territories of Bardez and Salsette, but had since been withdrawn, and that orders had been published for the ports to be opened, and for traders to be allowed to pass from place to place as heretofore; the Viceroy thereupon agreed to ratify anew the Treaties of the 29th January 1582 and the 3rd April 1633, and the Ambassador having, in the name of the Adil Shah, sworn to keep the peace, the Viceroy gave a similar undertaking on behalf of His Majesty the King of Portugal and his heirs.

Tratados, T. II., pp. 240–290.

In the second volume of Biker's "Collection of Treaties," there are a number of documents relative to the Treaty of Peace between England and Portugal of the 23rd June 1661, and the marriage of King Charles II. with the Infanta Donna Catharina. Under this Treaty the Island of Bombay was ceded to King Charles as part of the dowry of the Infanta.*

Tratados, T. III., p. 38.

On the 9th April 1662 the King of Portugal wrote to the Viceroy, Antonio de Mello e Castro, instructing

* There is in the Torre do Tombo an inventory of the possessions of Donna Catharina at the time of her marriage.

him to hand over the Island of Bombay to the English. Antonio de Mello reached Bombay from Lisbon on the 29th September, but refused to surrender the island, in explanation of which he wrote to the King on the 28th December :—

"It did not appear convenient to hand over Bombay, as the British refused me assistance every time I asked for it, and went so far as to hand over to the Moors of Anjuanne 42 of your Majesty's vassals, among which number there were 27 Christians which I had with me in the vessel. Your Majesty says in your letter, 'As soon as you arrive 'at the estate of India you shall demand the King's warrant, and 'thereby you will know the persons to whom the possession is to be 'given and the delivery made.' Abraham Shipman gave me, instead of the warrant which I asked for, a sealed letter written in Latin, and Letters Patent in English. The letter had defects, and the Letters Patent had not the signature of the King of England. I doubted the validity of the one and the other, as all the Letters Patent I have ever seen had the Royal signature; and there could be no reason for the omission in this case." . . . "If I doubted the letter which they call a warrant, how could I hand them over the place, as the conditions under which your Majesty's instructions were given were wanting?" . . . "The secret chapter which your Majesty sent me says, that the King of England agrees to arrange peace between your Majesty and the Dutch on honourable, advantageous, and safe terms for your Majesty, and, in the event of the Dutch not agreeing to the terms, he will send such a fleet as will defend and protect all the Portuguese possessions in India, and that this fleet shall be sent at the same time as the instructions for the handing over of Bombay are given. If your Majesty orders me to hand over Bombay in accordance with the terms of the capitulations, it follows that I cannot hand it over in another form. The terms of the capitulation require the King of England shall first arrange the treaty of peace; that the Dutch should first either agree to the terms or not and continue the war, and that a sufficient fleet should be sent to help us in the latter case. So that the King of England cannot take possession of Bombay. How can I give up Bombay? The treaty of peace is neither accepted nor refused, and no fleet has arrived.

"Moreover, I see the best port your Majesty possesses in India, with which that of Lisbon is not to be compared, treated as of little value only by the Portuguese themselves. I see in the Island of Bombay so many Christian souls which some day will be forced to change their religion by the English. How will they allow Catholics to reside in their territories when they hand Catholics over to the Moors? I considered also that your Majesty has no other place to receive and shelter your Majesty's ships. The English once there, and the island fortified, your Majesty will lose all to the north as they will take away all your Majesty's trade. The English are at peace with us now, but what would it be in case of war? How can those islands which are the granaries of India, once wedged in between the British and the Mogores, be defended?

"I have shown how I have obeyed your Majesty's orders by preserving the reputation of your Majesty's arms, and prevented the total loss and destruction of your Majesty's territories by not handing over Bombay. As a remedy for all the aforesaid there is only one thing, and that is for your Majesty to buy this island from the King of England. In another letter to your Majesty I say that your Majesty can give from 200 to 300,000* cruzados in three years; now I say your Majesty can give 500,000, 600,000, nay even 1,000,000† cruzados, and I undertake to say that all in this State, who would be pleased to be free from such a yoke, would assist in carrying out the arrangement."

In reply to the foregoing, the King of Portugal wrote on the 8th February 1664 as follows:—

"By your letter which has been brought to us overland by Manuel Godinho, I saw with great pain the difficulties which had arisen regarding the delivery of Bombay to the King of Britain, my brother and cousin. What, however, is stipulated in the capitulations admits of no doubt, and I trust that with your prudence you have now arranged matters so far that you will carry out my instructions at once. Should even fresh difficulties present themselves, I order you to overcome them. To the inhabitants of the place you must say they have misunderstood the Article of Capitulation shown them, as their goods will not be confiscated, but they will be allowed to remain in possession of them as heretofore. The difference will be that they will live under the dominion of the King of Great Britain, my brother, who will rule them with justice and in the freedom of the Roman Catholic religion, and with his power he will defend them and secure them in their trade. The King of England also undertakes to protect the places I have in that State, and this was one of the reasons I gave him that island. The inhabitants of the island are so allied by nationality, parentage, &c., to the Portuguese all over India that I consider the arrangement will be for their good. You must use all the means in your power to hand over the place soon, as this affair will not admit of delay. Immediately the delivery has taken place you will advise me, as it is of the utmost importance that it should be known here."

On receipt of the above letter, Antonio de Mello, learning that Sir Abraham Shipman was dead, addressed himself, on the 3rd November 1664, to the Supreme Court at Goa to the effect that, as the King of England had given a Commission to that officer to receive the Island of Bombay on His

Tratados, T. III., pp. 30, 32, 73.

* 25,000*l.* to 37,500*l.* † 62,500*l.*; 75,000*l.*, nay even 125,000*l.*

Majesty's behalf, and did not extend the power to any one else, he was at a loss to whom he should now surrender it. The Court replied that, having duly examined the will of Abraham Shipman and the Commission from the King of England, they were of opinion that the same powers were extended to Humphrey Cooque,* who had been nominated by Abraham Shipman by virtue of the said Commission, and that the island should be accordingly handed over to him. On receipt of this decision the Viceroy nominated a Commission consisting of Luis Mendes de Vasconcellos and Sebastião Alvares Nigos to carry out the decision of the Court in his name. This Commission left Goa on the 17th January 1665, reached Bombay on the 11th February, and handed over the island to Humfrey Cooke on the 18th idem. The English Governor requested the Commission to define the position of the territories of Bombay, and of the villages of Mazagão, Parella, Varoli, Maim, Sião, Daravi, and Vadala, but they replied that they were not instructed to hand over villages but the Island of Bombay, which, as was well known, lay surrounded by the sea; they did, however, define the positions of Mazagão, Parella, and Varoli, which belonged to the territory of the said island.

In a letter of the 5th January 1666 the Viceroy informed the King what had transpired since handing over the island, as follows:—

Tratados, T. III., p. 94.

"During the last monsoon I informed your Majesty I had handed over Bombay. Now I will relate to your Majesty what the English have done, and are doing every day in the way of excesses. The first act of Mr. Humphrey, who is the Governor of that island, and whom I knew in Lisbon as a grocer,† was to take possession of the Island of

---

* This was Mr. Humfrey Cooke, who had been Secretary to Sir Abraham Shipman.

† Sir George Oxenden, in a letter to George Stanian, dated Surat, 24th November 1666, referring to Cooke, remarked, "I am sorry to say he was once a pretender to be a merchant himself."—O. C., 3203.

Mahim in spite of my protests, the island being some distance from the Island of Bombay, as your Majesty will see from the map which I send herewith. He argues that at low tide one can walk from one to the other, and if this is conceded your Majesty will be unable to defend the right to the other northern island, as at low tide it is possible to go from Bombay to Salsette, from Salsette to Varagão, so that, in order not to lose the north, it will be necessary to defend Mahim. He has done more. He has obliged the Roman Catholics to take an oath by which they openly deny the jurisdiction of the Supreme Pontiff and Head of the Church. The inhabitants of the north would have taken up arms and driven out the English from thence if I had not had my suspicions and prevented them, by assuring them that your Majesty was actually in treaty about the purchase of Bombay. And, although the name of Humphrey Cooke appears in all these matters, an awful heretic named Henrique Guery, a great enemy of the Portuguese nation, is the author of all these things. I believe, however, that before your Majesty remedies this the Dutch will drive those people from thence, as I am told they are preparing a large armada to besiege Bombay.* Humphrey Cooke's replies to me have been full of boasting and bravado, but now they are humble and he asks for help. The State of India is not in a position to help any one, and were it so it would mean assisting the English against the Dutch, and, as an infallible consequence, your Majesty would lose everything in India. I have therefore ordered the north to be put in a state of defence before the Dutch arrive, and then to act as a friend of both parties. I repeat to your Majesty that it will be impossible to keep the little we have in India unless a great effort on the part of Portugal and England is made. This would have a great effect on the Dutch, who are sick and tired of everything."

---

* On the 2nd April 1666 the President and Council at Surat wrote to "Lieut. Governor" Cooke that nine Dutch ships of considerable burden were at that port, and that it was credibly reported that the Dutch General Rickloffe van Goens was coming with a great force shortly; his object could not be ascertained, but it was feared that an assault on Bombay was intended (O. C., 3164). Cooke replied on the 8th, stating that he was quite unprepared to meet such an assault, and that, should the island be lost, the blame would rest on them for refusing to supply him with money to hire soldiers and to buy provisions. He mentioned that ever since the preceding December, when he first heard the rumour of the Dutch designs, he had had forty "Portugalls of Europe" in pay, in addition to his own men (O. C., 3167). On the 17th the President and Council wrote again, that they had heard from the Dutch, "over a glass of wine," that Rickloffe's coming had been put off "by reason of the lateness of the year," and that on the 15th six of the Dutch ships had left for Batavia, and so their fears of an assault on Bombay were at an end (O. C., 3169).

Three years after the date of this letter the King wrote to the Viceroy (26th March 1669) informing him that he had received a representation from the Council of the Holy Office that the British in the Island of Bombay allowed everyone to live as he liked, but did not permit the Holy Office to carry on their work as they saw fit, by reason of which certain offenders against the faith remained unpunished. This, His Majesty argued, was against the capitulations agreed upon for the transfer of Bombay, and he stated that the Council had sent a protest through their Commissary at Bombay. In conclusion His Majesty desired that the orders of the Holy Office should be kept, and he commanded the Viceroy to make the necessary representations to the English in Bombay, in order that the said capitulations might be completely carried out. In reply the Viceroy informed the King, on the 24th January 1670, that he had written to the Governor of Bombay, but had received no reply as yet, "and do not expect one soon, "considering Henrique Gary* is now governing the "place." In another letter of 25th January 1670, he remarked :—

Tratados, T. III., p. 107.

Tratados, T. III., p. 114.

Tratados, T. III., p. 115.

"Henrique Gary, Governor of the Island of Bombay, is very astute, and an enemy of the Portuguese nation. He wishes that his vessels should be exempted from dues at our ports, and now asks us to pay dues on a frigate which came from Mombassa, and went *viâ* Bombay and discharged at Turumba, a village in the jurisdiction of Baçaim; we are considering the matter with due care, and we think that if these events as well as others had been forseen, this island would never have been handed over to the English."

On the 23rd March 1671 the King wrote to the Viceroy:—

Tratados, T. III., p. 118.

---

* The Governors of Bombay appointed by the Crown were Sir Abraham Shipman; his Secretary, Mr. Humfrey Cooke, who took possession of the island in 1665; Sir Gervase Lucas, who succeeded in 1666; and Captain Henry Gary, who officiated in 1667–68.

"As regards the second million* which has to be paid on account of the dowry of the Queen of Great Britain, my sister, the manner of payment has been settled between the Envoy, Robert Southwell, and the Marquis of Niza and Marialva, and in order that this matter may soon be settled it will be convenient if you send, per first monsoon, a detailed statement of the values of the estates of private individuals in Bombay."

In informing His Majesty that this information would take time to collect, the Viceroy added:—

"The Governor and the Ministers of His Majesty the King of England who are in Bombay are most insolent, they are so exorbitant and their demands so vexatious that the inhabitants have been obliged to leave their homes and go to Baçaim and Tanna; and when they complain under the capitulations, they are simply told they must send their complaints to the King of England, as the port is his. They are making a large and opulent city of the island, and as those who go there are those with open consciences our places and towns are being deserted. If your Highness does not take steps to remedy these evils, all the revenues and commerce of these inhabitants will be extinct, and they will be reduced to the utmost poverty as is the case now in Chaul."

Tratados, T. III., p. 133.

The following document appears in the Portuguese Records as proposals made by Gerald Aungier,† Governor of

* The following is an extract from Pepys' Diary of the 24th May 1662:—"My Lord (Sandwich) was forced to have some clash with the "Council of Portugal about payment of the portion before he could get "it, which was, besides Tangier and free trade in the Indys, two millions "of crowns, half now, the other half in twelve months. But they have "brought but little money, but the rest in sugar and other commoditys, "and bills of exchange."

† The Company's ship "Constantinople Merchant" reached Swally 1st September 1668, bringing a warrant from King Charles, addressed to Sir Gervase Lucas, ordering him to surrender Bombay to the Company, and also a commission from the latter to the President and Council of Surat and others, empowering them to take possession of the island. Two days later, at a consultation held in Surat under the presidency of Sir George Oxenden, it was resolved to depute Mr. John Goodier (second in Council), Captain Henry Young, and Mr. Streynsham Masters for this duty. These gentlemen embarked accordingly on the "Constantinople Merchant," and reached their destination on the evening of the 21st September, when Captain Young and Mr. Cotes were at once sent on shore with the King's letter. The next day was spent in preparation for the ceremony of transfer, and on Wednesday, the 23rd, the Com-

the Island of Bombay and President of the East India Company, to Senhor Luiz de Mendonça Furtado de Albuquerque, Conde de Lavradio and Viceroy of India:—

"1. On the part of the Company and the British Nation the said Gerald Aungier, Governor of Bombay, &c., undertakes conscientiously to observe and keep the articles of that happy peace which was ratified by the two Crowns in the year 1661, desiring also that the said Viceroy shall on his part, and on behalf of the King of Portugal do the same, and require the subjects of the Crown of Portugal to obey the said articles.

"2. Considering the interests of both nations to live in peace and be united in bonds of greater friendship, that an alliance be made between them, whereby the said Gerald Aungier on the part of the Company and the Nation, undertakes that the English shall assist the Portuguese in the event of their being at war against the Mogul, Sivaji, or any other Princes of India, the Portuguese to do the same should the English require any assistance.

"3. In order to give the reciprocal friendship more force, it shall be permitted to the English to establish factories in all the cities, towns, and villages in territories belonging to the Portuguese Crown in those parts of India and Asia, paying such moderate duties as His Excellency the Viceroy shall deem reasonable, and which commerce shall permit, because the British prefer to establish themselves in Portuguese ports rather than in those of the Native States; it being understood, of course, that the Portuguese Nation shall be permitted to trade with the English ports, and pay the same duties as shall be paid by the English at Portuguese ports.

"4. That no duties be charged on imports excepting at the port of arrival and landing, and that they be free of all tolls over rivers, bridges, &c., and that punishment be meted out to the Mandovis of Tanna and Caranjá for their unbearable insolence, and the exorbitant duties and taxes which they arbitrarily impose on the subjects of His Majesty the King of England, who shall be allowed to pass and repass, without hindrance, the rivers, &c., it being understood that the Portuguese shall enjoy the same privileges in the Port of Bombay, where they shall move freely and pay no duties or taxes excepting when their goods are landed."

---

missioners landed and solemnly took over charge from the officiating Governor, Captain Henry Gary. The island thus became *de facto* the property of the Company from that date, the formal grant having been signed on the 27th of the preceding March. Sir George Oxenden, President at Surat, became then Governor of Bombay. He was succeeded by Gerald Aungier as President at Surat and Governor of Bombay on the 14th July 1669 (*Bombay Selections from State Papers*, Vol. I., p. 224, and *I. O. Records, Surat Letters received*). The seat of the Presidency was not, however, removed to Bombay until the 2nd May 1687.

In sending these proposals home, the Viceroy advised the Prince Regent not to agree to them, pointing out, at the same time, the advantages to the Portuguese Crown and the inhabitants of the North which would ensue from the purchase of the Port of Bombay, which, although having only a revenue in "foros" of 7,000 pardaos, would relieve all the northern places from oppression.

Tratados, T. III., p. 137.

In consequence of the complaints by the British of the manner they were treated by the Portuguese, King Charles II. addressed a letter to the Viceroy on the subject, dated 10th March 1677, to which his successor, Dom Pedro de Almeida, replied as follows, in a letter of the 11th November of that year :—

Tratados, T. III., pp. 143 and 148.

"The Conde de Lavradio, whom I have just succeeded as Viceroy, has handed me the letter your Majesty was pleased to address to him regarding the question of the Mandovis of Caranjá and Tanna. The Moors give the name of 'Mandovis' to what we call Custom Houses. Caranjá was always the Custom House of the whole *terra firma*, and Tanna of the part of Galliana and Bumdi *terra firma* of the Moors, and Bombay of the district where everyone pays taxes in the form of the ancient 'foros' of the time of the Moorish dominion; and as the vassals of the Prince, my master, are not exempt from the payment of duties in Bombay, it does not seem right that the vassals of your Majesty should be exempt from paying duties in my Prince's dominions. As regards the 'passes,' we issue them to the Moors and Natives in the usual form."

It appears from a letter which the Viceroy wrote to the Prince Regent, on the 20th January 1679, that the Governor of the Island of Bombay had allowed the officials of his Custom House to demand payment of 100 xerafins in duties on a Portuguese vessel belonging to the port of Tanna, which had loaded at Caranjá, on the grounds that that port was within the jurisdiction of Bombay. It was decided to demand the repayment of the 100 xerafins, and, in the event of this not being complied with, the Governor of Bombay was to be informed that he would be held responsible

Tratados, T. III., p. 160.

for all loss or damage the Portuguese might sustain; and, without actually undertaking hostilities, it was decided to stop all supplies from entering Bombay from Portuguese territories. The Governor of Bombay, however, not only refused all satisfaction, but seized some Salsette vessels and forced the "Rendeiro do Tabaco" to pay duties to the English. The Viceroy further informed the Prince Regent that the British were carrying on things in a most insolent manner, impeding the navigation of the salt ships and others in the jurisdiction of Baçaim; forcing them to pay duties and anchorage dues; and doing the same to vessels of Bandora, Salsette, and Caranjá; allowing several persons charged with various crimes to remain in Bombay; assisting Arabian enemies with powder and arms; allowing certain Native Christians to return to heathenism; forbidding the Ministers of the Church to punish them; ordering crosses to be pulled down; and permitting the erection of pagodas for the heathen and mosques for the Moors. All these things being, as the Viceroy alleged, contrary to the capitulations, he suggested that the best way to settle all disputes would be for the King of Portugal and the King of England each to nominate a representative who should come to some agreement and remove all doubts as to the exact terms of the capitulations.

In another letter the Viceroy complained that the English had taken, and refused to give up, certain lands to which the priests laid claim in Bombay,* regarding which, it is stated, the English alleged they were not bound by the capitulations, having conquered those territories anew. The King accordingly directed him to continue to stop all supplies from reaching the English, as although they might have

Tratados, T. III., pp. 170 and 171.

* This must have reference to the mainland, and not the Island of Bombay.

sufficient for one year they would be unable to hold out longer, and thus become reduced to such straits as would compel them to grant what was wanted. "Experience has proved," His Majesty added, "on various occasions, when they have been denied supplies they have acted in all ways in a manner beneficial to our State, and the good of our vassals." In reply to this, however, the Viceroy said in a letter of the 19th December 1695:—

"These English, directly they become aware that we intend cutting off their supplies, suggest to the enemies that they make some demonstration against our territories, and this they generally do at a season before the crops are fit for gathering, when the inhabitants and vassals of Baçaim, frightened at the idea of war, and fearing they may lose their crops, send them to Bombay for safer custody and a better sale. Thus the British secure larger supplies than they require, and sell the surplus for high prices. This is not all the English do. They supply the enemy (the Arabs) with arms and ammunition, to the great danger of the State, which could scarcely defend itself against its Asiatic enemies."

Pombal MSS., 439, fol. 48.

In reply to this the King wrote, on the 1st March 1697:—

"Having noted what you write to me as regards the English in Bombay having sent the Arabs of Muscat powder, shot, and all other necessaries for the equipment of their ships, thus interfering with the peace negotiations which they contemplated entering into, in consequence of the losses inflicted on them by our frigates in 1693, and that they, the Arabs, had carried the British flag and employed British captains in order to avoid seizure, and to be enabled to carry contraband goods; in reply to your question as to what action you are to take in such cases, I would say that at any time that any of our enemy's ships are encountered under the command of English captains they should be seized. I would, however, recommend you to be cautious in these matters, and bear in mind the state of the weather and the forces at your disposal."

On the 14th February 1671 the King of Kanara, in a letter to the Viceroy, offered to give sites at Mangalor, Barcelor, and Onor for the erection of factories; but he stipulated that these should not be surrounded by double walls, but only by single walls, and that no embrasures or bastions should be erected

Tratados, T. IV., pp. 193 and 195.

thereon; also that no oil-mills should be started; that the native weights and measures should be employed; that no one was to be made a Christian against his will; and no Brahmins or cows were to be slain. The King also undertook to give the Portuguese every facility for trade, on payment of the customary duties; and in return for all these privileges he asked that the Portuguese should assist him with powder and shot against the Moors and others, and that they should undertake not to help his enemies or give them shelter. In reply the Viceroy stipulated that the factories should be such as to admit of artillery, but otherwise he agreed generally to the proposals, and suggested in addition that the King should compel all Christians living in his kingdom to obey the priests in everything, and that the practice of obliging them to worship in pagodas should be discontinued in future.

Tratados, T. IV., p. 207.

After this there would appear to have been an outbreak of hostilities against the Portuguese on the part of the King of Kanara, since in a Treaty of Peace, Alliance, and Commerce concluded with him on the 15th December 1678, His Majesty agreed to pay 30,000 xerafins towards the cost of wars, &c., and bound himself not to make any reference to the losses sustained in consequence of the capture of some of his ships by the Portuguese, whilst the latter also undertook not to demand payment of any overdue tributes or taxes, nor satisfaction for damages and losses caused to the State by the King of Kanara. The King further undertook to supply stone and wood for the erection of a factory at Mangalor; to pay annually, besides the tributes stipulated for at Mangalor and Barcelor, 1,500 sacks of clean rice; to pull down the existing factory belonging to the Arabs; not to allow them to trade in any way with his dominions, and not to send any of his ships to their ports.

I shall conclude this Section with extracts from two

letters from the Viceroy to the King, dated the 2nd January 1699 :—

"Francisco Pereira da Silva sailed from Baçaim in the frigate 'Nossa Senhora da Conceição,' accompanied by a fire-ship. The Admiral, Dom Antonio de Menezes, left Goa in the frigate 'Nossa Senhora da Gloria' to meet the former at Cape de Resolgate.* On the 13th May of this year (1698) these frigates met and sighted eight Arabian ships, who made for our ships with such determination that their flagship ran into the stern of our flagship. The intention of the enemy was, of course, to board us, but in this they were not successful as their spritsail got entangled with our ship, and the enemy lost 200 killed, including the Commander, who was the Baly of Mataré, and the chief officers. The two vessels were locked for three hours, during which time the musketry fire was most severe. The Arab ship eventually disengaged itself, and we gave it a parting broadside, whereupon the enemy fled. Our losses were 5 killed and 11 wounded."

Pombal MSS. 439, fol. 271.

"These seas are so overrun with Corsairs that commerce has been seriously damaged, and will be totally destroyed if it is allowed to continue. In March our ships encountered two pirate vessels, who robbed one of the Company's ships, and the frigate 'Conceição' had to go to Coulão for repairs. They took all the gold from the Company's ship, the men on board the Corsair's ships being chiefly composed of Englishmen, in fact, it is believed that all Englishmen are Corsairs, who sell in Bombay all they can steal at sea. If our frigates meet them at sea they produce the Company's papers, and we can do nothing with them; but when they come across our merchantmen they rob them, and the Company then excuse themselves by saying the ships are pirates."

Pombal MSS. 489, fol. 249.

* Cape Ras-el-Had in Arabia.

PORTUGUESE INDIA.

SECTION IV. 1700—1798.

The eighteenth century opened in India with favourable auspices for the Portuguese, whose flag was, about this time, again seen in the Persian Gulf; but the expectations raised by the alliance with the Shah of Persia were not fulfilled (*vide* Section "Red Sea and Persian Gulf.") The Viceroy Caetano de Mello de Castro signalized his administration by excessive energy. He had the fortress of the Bounsolo at Ambona demolished, and went in person to capture and destroy the stronghold of Bicholim in the year 1705. He also took and fortified the islands of Corjuem and Pondem in 1706. A successor, Vasco Fernandes Cesar de Menezes, having been insulted by the King of Kanara, went with a small squadron to Barcelor, and dismantled the fortress at that place, burnt the villages along the river banks, and killed all who offered an opposition. Calianapor, on the same coast, suffered a similar fate. After this he bombarded Mangalor, Comuta, Gocorna, and Mirzes, spreading terror, fire, and death in every direction.

The documents relating to Portuguese India during the 18th century are very voluminous, and it would be impossible to give even brief references to the events they record without entering into too great length for a report of this nature. It is proposed, therefore, to limit the present section to little more than a brief outline of the principal events which occurred during that century between the Portuguese and the Mahrattas and the pirate Angria respectively.

On the 13th January 1717 Dom Sebastião de Andrade

Pessanha, the Archbishop and Primate of India, on the departure of the Viceroy for Lisbon, took over the reins of government which he held for three months. During this time the Mahrattas made an incursion into the province of Salsette, and a body of 500 horse rode through the district without meeting with any opposition, sacking the different towns, and retired carrying with them loot to the extent of 400,000 xerafins, chiefly in silver, besides several sacred ornaments from the churches. On the succession of Dom Luis de Menezes, the Conde da Ericeira, as Viceroy, he prepared a fleet of five vessels which he despatched against an Arab fleet from Muscat which had appeared off Diu and Damão. This fleet went first to Surat in order to prevent the Arabs from leaving their ports, and then proceeded to Por-patam, a strong port not far from Diu, and which for 19 years had neglected to pay the annual sum of 2,000 xerafins to the State, which it was under an obligation to do, in consideration of passports being issued to its ships by the authorities at Diu. On arrival there the commander sent to demand from the Divan of Por-patam the then overdue tribute, and gave him a few days within which to pay it. This interval, however, the authorities made use of in preparing for defence, and the commander receiving no reply landed a force on the 31st December 1717. After several unsuccessful attempts, the place was taken by storm and the defenders retired to a stronghold. The city was reduced to cinders, and all the boats on the shore were destroyed. In this engagement the Portuguese lost a little over 80 men, including several officers, whilst the loss of the enemy exceeded 1,500 killed and wounded. The Porpatanes then gave hostages for the payment of the 38,000 xerafins which they owed, and agreed to conditions of peace.

Bibliotheca Publica MSS., Vol B., 6–17, fols. 98 to 159.

In the year 1718 an engagement took place, off

Angediva, between four of Angria's* vessels and two Portuguese ships which were convoying some merchantmen; after a stubborn fight the enemy was defeated and retired. In the same year the kings of Assarceta and Ramanaguer† invaded the villages of Damão, capturing cattle and taking the cultivators of the soil prisoners. A Portuguese force went in pursuit and drove the invaders before them as far as Fatapar,‡ which place they burnt, but they were unable to save

---

* Kanoji Angria, the son of Tukoji, a Mahratta Chief of the family of Angria, first attained eminence in the service of the Raja of Satara about the year 1698, and subsequently distinguished himself in the war in the Konkan carried on by the Mahrattas against that portion of the Mahomedan dominions. Taking advantage of his own power, and of the dissensions in the Satara family, he attempted to make himself independent, and succeeded so far as to retain in his possession the whole of the seaports from Viziadrug to Kolaba.. Thence his fleets crept out to plunder indiscriminately the vessels both of native traders and of European merchants, and for half a century the Angria pirates were a terror in the Bombay seas. After Kanoji's death the sovereignty reverted first to his eldest son Sakoji, then to his second son Sambhaji, and finally to his third son Tulaji, with whom the power of the dynasty came practically to an end. The Bombay Government, who had previously endeavoured on several occasions to dislodge this horde of pirates, but without success, determined, in 1755, to make a renewed effort, and in March of that year despatched Commodore James with an expedition for this purpose. Suvarndrug and Bankot were captured, and a demonstration was made against Ratnagiri; but the final blow to Tulaji's power was not delivered until February in the following year, when a fleet under Admiral Watson, with a land force commanded by Lieut.-Col. Clive, bombarded and captured Gheria (Viziadrug), his chief stronghold. Tulaji fell into the hands of the Peishwa, who was acting in conjunction with the British; and the power of the Angrias came virtually to an end. Their piracies occasionally gave trouble down to the Treaty of Bassein (1802), after which they ceased altogether, while the family of the once powerful chieftains dwindled gradually into insignificance.

† Assarceta, or Sarceta, five leagues to the north of Daman. The king of this place was named Virgire or Virgi. Ramanaguer is the name of a range of hills not far from Chaul; it would appear from the context in the Portuguese Records that the King of Ramanaguer was named Choutia.

‡ Fatapar, or Fatehpur, a city in the State of Dharampor, not far from the frontier of Daman.

the captives. The king in his flight fell from his horse and was killed. His nephew, who succeeded him, sued for peace, which was accordingly agreed to.

During the year 1721, the Viceroy, Dom Francisco José de Sampaio, made preparations for a vigorous attack on Angria, and invited the assistance of the British, of whose vessels that pirate had made several prizes of late. Charles Boone, the Governor of Bombay, sent Robert Corran to Goa to make arrangements as to the conditions of alliance. He arrived there on the 20th August 1721, when he concluded a treaty under which the British* undertook to supply 2,000 men and five small

---

* The Report on this transaction, which must have been sent home, is not now in existence amongst the Indian Office Records. The following account is taken from a history of the wars with Angria, written by Clement Downing, an officer of the ship "Salisbury," which was engaged in the attack on that pirate. In consequence of a representation by the Court of Directors of the East India Company to the King and Council with reference to Angria, His Majesty appointed a squadron of men-of-war, under the command of Commodore Matthews, consisting of the "Lyon," the "Salisbury," the "Exeter," and the "Shoreham," to assist the Honourable Company's Settlements, and to suppress pirates and robbers infesting the Indian seas. This fleet arrived at Bombay in October 1721. The President determined on an attack on Allibeg and invited the Portuguese Viceroy to lend his assistance, which he did, and took the command of the Portuguese forces himself. The English forces were placed under the command of Mr. Cowing. The united forces, consisting of about 5,000 men, started from Chaul, whence they marched to Allibeg, and the English commander arranged the army in order of attack, having the Portuguese on the right wing and the English seamen on the left. The day of attack having arrived, the Viceroy of Goa went on board his ship on the plea that he was taken very ill. The Commodore sent his own doctor to him, to offer his service and supply him with such medicines as might be necessary, but he returned and reported to the Commodore that he did not perceive anything to be the matter with the Viceroy. On the appointed day the whole army advanced to the attack with scaling ladders, "whereupon the Angrians came down in a great body, "with several elephants, which the general of the north perceiving he "broke the order of his wing; and the seamen being employed in "storming the castle (which for certain they would have taken had they "been properly supported) the whole army fell into confusion. So soon "as the enemy saw that the Portuguese were on the retreat, and the

ships. Culabo, when taken, was to be the property of Portugal, and the fortress of Griem, 30 leagues to the north of Goa, was to be handed over to the English. A few days before the treaty of alliance was concluded, the Angria wrote to the General of the North, Dom Antonio de Castro e Mello, to say that he was aware of the understanding between the Portuguese and the British, and was determined to resist them, for which purpose he had 20,000 troops of his own, besides those of relations and allies, and that they had, therefore, better settle any differences amicably. He accused the Portuguese of having always provoked war, and asserted that he had never done anything else but defend himself. This letter only made the Viceroy hasten his preparations for war; and the Angria, in spite of his alleged desire to avoid hostilities, continued to fortify his sea ports, especially that of Culabo.

The Viceroy sailed from Goa on the 22nd November 1721 with a fleet of four ships and six smaller vessels, and arrived on the 1st December at Chaul, where he landed munitions of war for the defence of that place. On the 9th the Portuguese force arrived at the camp of Madre de Dios, near Chaul, where troops had already been gathering from the northern provinces, and the

---

" whole army was confused, they came down upon them and made a " terrible slaughter amongst the English soldiers and seamen ; great " part of our army was taken, with most of the ammunition thereto " belonging. The whole army was now on the rout, and the Com- " modore came on shore in a violent rage, flew at the general of the " north and thrust his cane in his mouth, and treated the Viceroy not " much better. Thus the Angrians defeated us this time, entirely by " the treachery of the Portuguese, who seemed to design only to lead " our people on and then to leave them in the lurch ; this seemed the " more probable, for they never once offered to pursue them, but let them " march off without any molestation. We got off most of our scattered " forces, and what part of the baggage and artillery we had saved, " and re-embarked, though we had great numbers killed and wounded."

It appears from the Portuguese Records that the Angria was, in 1725, at peace with the Portuguese, and had returned to the British the prisoners he had made on several occasions. *Bibliotheca Publica MSS.*, Vol. B., 6–17, fol. 40.

Viceroy's army now amounted to 5,597 infantry and 125 horse. The English fleet of nine sail, which co-operated in this movement, was commanded by Thomas Matthews.

On the 16th December the force crossed the river Ragaçaim, and encamped on some heights on the other side. Here they remained until the 20th, when the enemy, making a flank movement, delivered an attack and killed some soldiers, but were quickly repulsed by the Portuguese artillery. On the 21st, the Portuguese forces marched, under the protection of their guns, to a camp on the river Alibaga, and pushed on thence to just outside the range of the guns of Culabo. Here the enemy had entrenched themselves, and on the 22nd the Viceroy moved up the river and encamped on the heights within range of the enemy, whereupon an artillery duel commenced. On the 23rd, the Angria's army marched as if to attack the Portuguese position, but was driven back by the heavy fire of their artillery. On the 24th the English General, Robert Curran, marched with 500 men to the gates of the city, and after throwing 180 grenades into the place retired towards the river. On the 28th, the Portuguese camp was strengthened by means of a palisade, and on the 29th some skirmishing took place. The Viceroy was now taken ill, and, on the advice of his doctors, went on board his ship, leaving the command to Dom Antonio de Castro e Mello and Robert Curran. On the 30th, the Angria was reinforced by 6,000 horse, which were sent to him by Bagi Rao.

On the 1st January 1722, the General, Bagi Rao, sent word that San Raja, his lord, was a friend of the Portuguese, and that he really had no intention of assisting the Angria against them, although it was his duty to help his vassals; all he wished for now was that the Viceroy and the Angria should come to terms and conclude a peace. The Viceroy, perceiving he could do nothing against the enemy, who had such a superior force in point of numbers, listened to this proposal, and agreed to a cessation of hostilities pending negotiations, each party handing over to the other five officers as hostages.

After a conference lasting several days, an agreement was concluded to the effect that all the territories under the Portuguese crown should be exempted from tribute, either to the Angria or to the Mahrattas; that assistance should be mutually rendered by the one to the other whenever required; and that all vessels seized by either party should be returned. This document was dated from the camp of Alibaga, the 12th January 1722.

This agreement, it was stipulated, was to be also binding on the English nation, as an ally of the Portuguese, and was to be ratified by them within eight days. The ships set sail on the 17th January. The Portuguese fleet carried the Viceroy to Goa, where he arrived on the following day. The Governor of Bombay sailed soon after for England, and was attacked *en route* by some of the Angria's ships, which he drove off, and would have captured had not night set in.

After this treaty, peace continued between the Portuguese and the Angria. The celebrated Kanoji Angria died in his fort of Culabo on the 20th June 1729, leaving two sons. In 1731 Kanoji's son recommenced his depredations by taking three ships from Damão, and he had the audacity to inform the Captain of Chaul that all other Portuguese ships would be similarly treated. About this time a frigate and some smaller vessels arrived at Verseva with 150 infantry and a similar number of sepoys, who at once marched to the Vaos, or Tanna Passes, where they found the British, who had only returned to Bombay on the 20th January, in consequence of the necessity of holding that island as a base of operations against the Angria, the common enemy. Early in April 1731, the Angria contemplated making an attack on some English ships which were on the bar of Culabo, whereupon the Governor of Bombay requested that the Portuguese ships there should join with the British vessels, and that the united fleets should act under the British commander. This was agreed to, and the projects of the Angria were thus frustrated.

In 1734 Dom Luiz Botelho was appointed General of the North, and he took over the command at Baçaim on the 8th May. His first project was to construct a fleet of small vessels for the defence of the coast against the depredations and insults of the Angria, who forced the fishermen to pay a certain tribute to him for permission to carry on their business in peace. To this end he demanded a heavy tribute from these same fishermen in order to provide the necessary funds. The demand was, however, considered an act of great injustice by the fishermen, and the collection of the tax had, in many cases, to be carried out by means of force. Six galleys were thus built, but they soon proved to be useless as they only made one voyage down the coast, and speedily became unseaworthy.

Fol. 91.

Samanagi (? Sambhaji) Angria having taken the fortress of Chaul de Sima (called the Casa Branca, or White House) from the Sidi in 1735, and having garrisoned it with 400 foot and 2,000 Mahratta horse, knowing the jealousy with which the Portuguese looked upon the presence of such a force in their neighbourhood, tried to persuade the Governor that the garrison of Culabo had risen against him, and that he had merely gone for shelter to Chaul with 200 faithful followers, assuring him that it was his intention to hand over the fortress to him. The General, on hearing this news, immediately wrote to the Governor urging him to take all necessary steps to have the Samanagi arrested. Orders were issued accordingly, and a serjeant-major was sent with 250 men to occupy a neighbouring mosque. In this he was not successful and had to retire; but on the

Fol. 94A.

following day he returned with a force of 1,500 men and two guns, and laid siege to the place for 22 days, during which several attempts were made to carry it by storm, but in vain. He had finally to retire with a loss of 22 killed and 30 wounded, whilst the enemy's loss was 108. The differences between the Angria and the Portuguese were eventually settled through the mediation of the Governor of Bombay.

The island of Karanja had been often menaced by Samanagi Angria, who had always had designs on that place. About the year 1739, when the Portuguese were occupied with the Mahratta forces, he thought it a good opportunity to organise an expedition against the island. He accordingly collected together 40 vessels well armed, and landed a force of 2,000 men together with some guns and mortars, with which he attacked the fortress with such energy and determination that it surrendered on the 28th March after a siege of five days. The besieged only lost three killed and some wounded out of a garrison of 100 men. After this the Angria entertained designs against Chaul, which place he besieged at the end of March, with 800 men and three guns. The Governor sent Perseval Machado with a force to attack him from the side of the sea, and Captain Miguel Pereira with 200 men of the Chaul garrison, to attack him from the land side. The action took place on the 1st April, and was most successful. The enemy's position was entered, the three guns were spiked, and 60 of the Angria's men were killed. The enemy, having received reinforcements, erected new batteries which they armed with 15 guns, with which they kept up a heavy fire, but without doing much harm, so they turned their attention to the capture of the fort on the hill (Forte do Morro) which commanded the bar, and formed a camp in its vicinity. The Governor determined to dislodge the enemy, and

Fol. 168A.

Fol. 180.

accordingly on the 5th April he embarked with a force of two companies of grenadiers and 100 irregulars. He disembarked on the quay of the fortress at midnight and joined the garrison. On the 6th, the Governor attacked a church where the enemy had fortified themselves, when the latter were thoroughly routed losing their guns, 80 killed, and a large number of wounded, besides 19 prisoners. The losses on the Portuguese side were 7 killed and 22 wounded. Driven from this position the enemy made preparations for fortifying their camp at Chaul, whence they advanced day by day until they had made an entrenchment only 60 paces from the Portuguese works. In consequence of the arrival of Manoel Caetano de Souza Ferreira, the newly appointed Commander of the armies of the north, the Angria raised siege on the 18th October, and retired with his forces.

In the following year (1740) doubts began to be entertained as to the advisability of retaining Chaul, owing to the difficulty experienced in providing means for its defence. The preceding year it had been offered to the Dutch, on the occasion when their fleet called at Goa, but nothing was then done owing to the Commander not possessing the necessary powers. There was little hope entertained that the English would buy the place, as the East India Company was nearly ruined, and almost compelled to leave Bombay owing to the heavy expenses they were obliged to incur not being made up by trade, in consequence of the numerous captures at sea by the Angria. It did not therefore appear likely that they would care to occupy Chaul and so become nearer neighbours to the Angria's brother. However, Captain Francisco Xavier de Vasconcellos, who was accompanied by Luiz de Mello Pereira, proceeded to Bombay to treat of the matter, and in case he should not effect the sale in the manner proposed, he was to offer part of the artillery of Chaul in payment of the loan obtained for the subsidy of the troops which had been in the island.

On the 5th November 1755, the Portuguese Viceroy entered into a treaty with Tulaji Angria, by which he undertook to assist the latter with 500 men in the war he was then engaged in with Bellagi Bagi Rao, and the Angria engaged to pay them out of his treasury at the same rate paid by the Portuguese. The terms of this treaty were evidently not faithfully kept by the Angria, since on the 29th January 1756 the Viceroy addressed to him the following letter :—

Tratados, Vol. VII., fols. 36, 45.

"I have received your letter in which you call attention to the recall of the troops which I sent to the assistance of the cities which were menaced by the Mahrattas. The Commander committed no act worthy of punishment, inasmuch as the Commander and officers, as well as the naval captain, Ismal Can, inform me that there has been a breach of faith on your part in not keeping some of the stipulations agreed upon; and as the Commander had instructions to see that these stipulations were duly carried out, he preferred to retire with the escort to this city (Goa) rather than be mixed up in any hostilities which might break out."

Notwithstanding that the power of the Angria was practically now broken on land (*see note p.* 79), the representatives of that family still exercised no inconsiderable amount of power on the seas, since on the 7th January 1778 the Portuguese entered into a treaty with Ragogi Angria, who called himself "Lord of Culabo," in accordance with which firm friendship was declared to exist between the contracting parties; the vessels of Culabo were to be permitted free commerce with Goa, Damão, and Diu, provided they were furnished with passports by the Angria, and all Portuguese vessels carrying the Viceroy's passports were to be free to trade with the ports of Culabo. The fleets of the two powers, if in distress, were to be allowed free entry to their respective ports to refit, where they were to be supplied with all necessaries at reasonable prices; and, in the event of either party requiring assistance, it was to be furnished by the other on demand.

Tratados, Vol. VIII., fol. 47.

The commencement of the 18th century witnessed the Mogul empire crumbling to pieces before the irresistible assaults of the Mahrattas, and after the death of Aurungzebe, on the 21st February 1707, a great development was given to the progress of the Mahratta power. On several occasions the Portuguese had attacked Mahratta strongholds, and in 1731 the Mahratta forces retaliated and sent a body of troops down the ghauts against them. On receipt of the news of this invasion at Goa, the Viceroy sent the ship "Madre de Dios" with troops which were distributed amongst the threatened ports. On the 27th February a body of 2,000 Mahratta infantry and 500 horse made its appearance before Manora, and on the 1st March they had gained possession of the neighbourhood, and cut off the water that supplied the garrison. Reinforcements reached the garrison on the 5th March, whereupon the enemy retired with their guns to their camp. On the morning of the following day, a force of 170 Portuguese marched out and attacked the enemy (who occupied a strong position in the village of Amboana) with such determination that they fled, leaving all their baggage behind them. Shortly after this, the Mahratta forces retired altogether from the neighbourhood, and a treaty was concluded at Baçaim on the 3rd July between Rago Panta and the Governor of the North, in which it was stipulated that the losses on either side were not to be referred to; that the Mahrattas should evacuate all the territories occupied by them in the Northern Provinces; and return all the artillery taken from the Portuguese; that all prisoners should be exchanged without any ransom; and that the Portuguese should return two merchant ships laden with salt, together with any others they might have captured during the war.

Bibliotheca Publica MSS., Vol. B., fol. 81.

Rago Panta left Baçaim immediately for Galliana (Galna) with the understanding that he was to return with the ratification of the Treaty. But when he did come back seven days afterwards, he brought with him, in place of the ratification, some new proposals too preposterous to be granted, and he was ordered by the General to be imprisoned, as it was concluded that this evasion was intended only to gain time until the result of the war between San Raja and the Great Mogul should be ascertained. The Portuguese therefore carried on hostilities with greater energy than ever during the months of June, July, and August. On the 2nd October a force of 208 Portuguese and 562 Sepoys arrived at Turumba, with instructions to attack the village of Panuel, one of the chief places of the Mahrattas, which, after a brief resistance, was captured and burnt. Representatives of the Portuguese and of San Raja arrived in Bombay on the 17th January 1732 with the object of arranging a peace between them.

Bibliotheca Publica MSS., Vol. B., 6—17, fol. 97.

The construction of the fortress of Tana was still in progress in the year 1737, although it had been originally contemplated that twelve months would have sufficed for the purpose, and four years had now elapsed since its foundation. This delay caused great discontent to the people of that town, besides which those employed in its erection were unpaid and unfed. The latter were at last driven to such desperation that they invited the Mahrattas to take possession of the Island of Salsette, preferring the rule of those barbarians to their present persecutions and oppressions. The Mahrattas, who had been only waiting for a suitable opportunity, considered that this had now arrived, and one Pantagi Panta, a Mahratta General, proceeded to Galliana Biundi, a Mahratta place five leagues distant from the Island of Salsette, with a body of troops which he gradually increased until he had collected a force of 12,000 men, of both infantry and cavalry. News of this collection of Mahratta forces was communicated to the General of Salsette, but he refused to believe it, and made no preparation to resist it. Accordingly, at 4 o'clock in the morning of the 6th April, 100 of the enemy crossed over at low tide and captured the fortress of St. Jeromino with scarcely any resistance, and these were speedily followed by 500 more men. The General, being thus taken by surprise, was unable to offer any effectual resistance, and, after a consultation with his officers, he abandoned the island and retired with all his forces to Karanjá. The enemy soon took possession of all the forts in Salsette; they sacked the places, destroyed the churches, and did other damage without losing a single man or firing a shot.

On the following day the enemy marched to the fort of Varsevá, with a force of 500 soldiers, thinking it was only garrisoned by 15 men, but they were repulsed with heavy loss. At the same time they attacked the house at Bandorá, a college of Jesuits, which successfully resisted the attack with the aid of some British who were in the pay of that order, and the enemy was forced to retire.

The General having sent reinforcements from Karanjá to Varsevá and Bandorá, proceeded to Baçaim, which he found blockaded. In the neighbourhood of the latter place the enemy had stationed a force ready to enter Casabé directly the Island of Salsette should be captured. They, being informed by their spies of what had occurred in Salsette, crossed the river Gocarvem, one league from Casabé, on the night of the 6th April, and took that place by surprise. The Portuguese forces fled to the Ilha das Vaccas, and, not feeling secure there, passed on to Bombay. The enemy, following them closely up, immediately took possession of the island, which they commenced to fortify, and, had they continued their march straight on to Baçaim, that city would have been placed in a position of great danger.

On the morning of the 7th the captain of the place marched with a company of grenadiers, and four other companies of natives, to reconnoitre the enemy's camp, and were met by a force of 1,000 horse and 2,000 infantry. The Portuguese engaged them for an hour, but were obliged to retire to the fortress, and then made all the necessary preparations for its defence. In the afternoon, the enemy entered Casabé, and immediately began to erect earthworks in the direction of Madrapor. They then attacked the fortress of Parsica, which only resisted for two days, the captain and force who defended it, after spiking the guns, escaping one night to Baçaim. The neighbouring fort of Trangipará, which was defended by an ensign, resisted with great valour several attacks, and, after the few soldiers which composed the garrison were killed, he gave himself up as a prisoner of war, and eventually escaped from the enemy. A worse fate befell those who abandoned the Ilha das Vaccas, as their ships were attacked and seized by some of the Angria's vessels, and they lost everything.

Having taken the six forts in the Island of Salsette, the enemy then proceeded to attack the fortress of Sabajo, which capitulated on the 7th May after several days hard fighting.

On the same day that Sabajo surrendered, the enemy again attacked the fortress of Varsevá at seven in the morning. In this they were not successful, as, although they got close to the walls, they were completely repulsed by the defenders, and lost heavily in killed. The Portuguese losses were one killed, and the commander seriously wounded. The enemy also sent a force of 3,000 men from Madrapor to besiege the fort of Saibana, which was under the command of the Captain Mor José de Miranda, who capitulated on the 13th day of the siege. There was, it is stated, no reason for the capitulation, as the fort had a plentiful supply of provisions and ammunition. The news of the surprise in the Island of Salsette and the loss of the fort of Taná, caused great and widespread consternation in Goa. The Governor and Viceroy determined on sending assistance to the Northern Provinces, and collected 200 men and 150,000 xerafins in cash. These were sent from Goa on the 18th April in the frigate "Nazareth," which, after a short voyage, reached Baçaim on the 26th or 28th of the same month.

Antonio Cardim was now appointed General of the Northern Provinces. He sailed from Agoada on board a British ship on the 18th May, and arrived at Baçaim on the 23rd of the same month, taking over the government on the following day. A few days previously, the enemy had fortified themselves on the top of the Agoada Hill, near an old fort which the Portuguese had formerly founded there. The General, being desirous of inaugurating his governorship by a noteworthy deed, determined on driving them from this position, so attacked them with 300 men on the morning of the 26th May, and, meeting with a very little resistance, gained the heights, the Mahrattas retreating and leaving several killed and wounded behind. The Portuguese loss was one killed and three wounded. Manora was at this time besieged by the same enemy, and, after a lengthened siege, capitulated. Bandorá was next attacked, but without success, and the enemy retreated from before it on the 5th June.

This conquest was the only one the enemy required to complete the glorious campaign of that summer, being the only check to their successful career, in which they had conquered the Island of Salsette and all its forts, and Manorá, Saibana, Sabajo, the forts of Paršica, the Ilha das Vaccas, the hills of Santa Cruz, and of Santa-Maria, which surrendered after a three days' siege. These successes encouraged the Mahrattas to proceed to further hostilities, and, on the 1st July, they again attacked the fort of Varsevá with 2,000 men, but not meeting with any success they retired. They then turned their attention to Baçaim. On the morning of the 8th July, with 4,000 men, they sallied forth from Madrapor with the intention of carrying Baçaim by storm. The Portuguese fire was, however, so severe that they were forced to retire with a loss of over 200 men. On the 15th September the enemy returned to the attack with 6,000 picked foot soldiers and 4,000 horse. They made several most determined onslaughts for an hour and a half, but were received by the defenders with such a hot fire, and suffered such severe losses, that they saw the futility of continuing the contest, and retired, leaving 120 killed near the walls, besides a number of wounded whom the General caused to be looked after and their wounds attended to. The defenders' losses were 6 killed and 15 wounded; they also captured 45 ladders.

The enemy had placed Tana in such a state of defence that it was almost hopeless to recover it, whilst Baçaim was in semi-state of siege, and the enemy had a force of 30,000 veteran soldiers commanded by Samanagi Apá, a brother of Bagi Rao, Commander-in-Chief of all the armies of San Rajá. It was considered of the utmost importance, therefore, to prepare for a rigorous and well planned defence, and, in order to carry this out, it was proposed to abandon the forts of Maym, Trapor, Aserim, Quelmé, Secredão, Danu, and Bandorá, which were incapable of resisting a siege, and to destroy them, retaining only Baçaim, Damão, Chaul, and Dio.

The Viceroy would not, however, listen to such proposals, as he did not consider it right to give up even an inch of land to any one. He was of opinion that they should hold on as long as they could. His opinion prevailed, and an additional force of 1,500 paid sepoys was raised for the purpose of defence.

Owing to the pressing necessities of the campaign, Goa was entirely denuded of troops, and remained with only a few friars, some fishermen, and a small number of black men to defend it. The whole available force there numbering some 300 Europeans and 1,300 sepoys, having been sent to the north on the 26th January, marched to Asserim. These arrived the following day, and the enemy, retiring from the neighbourhood at their approach, and fearing the Portuguese would make a descent on Manorá, abandoned that fortress, demolishing the works they had erected there. This force then proceeded to Baçaim, which place they entered without opposition.

The enemy were fortified in Dongrim, and the General deemed it advisable to attack them there. One of the strongholds near the church was easily captured, and in it were found large quantities of ammunition and provisions. The stronghold on the hill was next taken without much fighting. The town was then assaulted, and, after an hour's fighting, the enemy were completely routed.

General Antonio Cardim, finding it impossible to procure the necessary funds for carrying on the war, and seeing the impossibility of doing anything without money to pay his troops, now tendered his resignation, which was accepted, and he was succeeded by Pedro de Mello as General of the Northern Provinces.

The new General began his government to the satisfaction of everyone, and reduced the number of sepoys to 500 chosen men. He sent a force to engage the enemy at Madrapor, which defeated them with a loss of 60 killed, the sepoys only losing two killed and 15 wounded.

In the beginning of July the enemy took possession of the village of Danda Catal with 2,000 men, where they constructed a fortress with such celerity that they completed it before the end of the winter.

News having reached Lisbon (*viá* England) of the loss of Salsette, two ships were hastily equipped, and these, with 480 picked men, sailed from Lisbon at the end of April of the same year, and arrived at Goa safely. The Viceroy now resolved to re-conquer the fort of Tana, and for this purpose a fleet was prepared and started for the North on the 1st November, arriving at Chaul in 26 days, and, leaving some ammunition at that place, reached Baçaim on the 29th of that month. On the 4th December, the General of Baçaim left with 8 ships and 30 small craft, accompanied by 400 picked men and 600 sepoys, and made his appearance off Tana on the 6th *idem*. Being unable to get near enough to take the place by storm, he shelled it for two days, but with no success. He was, however, killed by a shot from the enemy, whereupon the fleet retired to Baçaim. Martinho da Silveira de Menezes now succeeded as General.

The death of General Pedro de Mello inspired the enemy with such pride that Samanagi Apá thought of nothing but the conquest of Baçaim. Having made the necessary arrangements, he ordered Sancragi Panta to cross the Ghats, and, in the beginning of November, began his march at the head of 8,000 foot and 10,000 horse, with which he entered the jurisdiction of Damão and sacked every place, then marched on to the defences of Catravará, which he conquered, and subsequently captured the forts of Humbargão, Nargol, and Danú. This accomplished, he joined the forces of Casabé, Agasaym, and Madrapor. Sancragi was afterwards sent to besiege Maym, which place capitulated on the 18th January 1739.

The loss of Maym was speedily followed by capture of the forts of Quelmé and Seridão.

The enemy then proceeded with their forces to Trapor, which place they attacked with 30 cannon, and, on the seventh day, gained an entrance, taking it by storm, and putting everybody to the sword. From thence they proceeded to Asserim, which they besieged for four days, and forced it to surrender on the 13th February.

On the 20th January 1739, news was received in Goa

that the enemy was only two days march from that place, and that he would soon be in Salsette. This caused great alarm, as the city was quite unprepared for defence. On the 26th the enemy entered the province, and was soon at the gates of Margão, and also of Rachol. The sound of artillery was heard during the afternoon and night of that day.

The forces then in Goa were the Viceroy's bodyguard of 35 men, a company of infantry in the island of Sancto Estevão, 180 seamen, 200 principais,* 500 friars, and some Kanarese auxiliaries, in which very little confidence could be placed. In Bardez there was a company of 60 grenadiers and a company of light infantry, a very small force indeed for the defence of such an extent of walls, especially as that province was menaced by the Bounsuló, who was then at Alorna with 2,200 horse.

The enemy with a force of 3,000 horse and 6,000 infantry encamped near Margão, whence they sent out small detachments to pillage the neighbouring villages, and seized quantities of cattle and provisions. They then attacked the fort and soon gained an entrance, the defenders surrendering on condition of their lives being spared. They next attacked Rachol, but, on reinforcements reaching that place, they were compelled to raise the siege, and retired from before it on the 6th May.

The Mahrattas had heard rumours that Baçaim had capitulated on the 14th May. These rumours proved correct. On the 10th May the enemy collected a large number of vessels to send to the island of Ivem; three days afterwards mines were fired close to Baçaim and a general attack on the place was made. On the 13th some vessels from Gorobandal hove in sight, and while those in Baçaim were watching them three mines were fixed near the bastion of Remedios, the result being a breach

---

* This is probably intended for Sipaes (Sepoys).

large enough to admit 20 men abreast. The enemy mado two furious attacks at this place, but were repulsed with heavy loss. More mines were fired near the bastion of San Sebastião, but did not cause much damage. The enemy made several determined assaults during this day, viz.,—six on the Remedios bastion, and fourteen on that of San Sebastião, but were repulsed each time with heavy loss. The Portuguese losses were very heavy, and as the garrison was but small compared with the attacking force, and the ammunition was running short, the captain of the place decided to make terms with the Mahrattas. On the morning of the 14th he sent a sepoy, with a flag of truce, to ask the enemy to receive some representatives in his camp for the purpose of arranging terms. This was granted. Terms of surrender were then agreed to, and signed on the 16th May 1739, and were as follows :—

All the regular and auxiliary troops to leave the place with arms loaded and flags unfurled. All the families and people in the place to be allowed a free exit, with all their property and goods. All the ships in the place, with their artillery, &c., to be permitted to leave. The families of all classes to be conveyed to Bombay, Damão, or Chaul. All the priests and others of religious orders who do not desire to remain in the place not to be prevented from leaving. All Christians electing to remain to be allowed to worship God in the manner of their religion. All prisoners to be exchanged. On the day the Captain and his troops evacuate the place the enemy to retire to Madrapor. The day for the evacuation to be Saturday the 23rd of May. The said Samanagi Apá not to enter the place until the Captain and his soldiers and others are on board and beyond the range of his guns.

The said Samanagi Apá, as long as he is in possession of Baçaim, to maintain three churches, viz., one at Baçaim, one at Casabé, and another in the island of Salsette.

The besieged left on the 23rd May, with all th honours and formalities agreed to.

On the departure of the Portuguese from Baçaim the enemy took possession of that place, and testimony is borne to the fact that they faithfully observed all the conditions of the capitulations, permitting all who wished to remain there in peace.

The losses to the Portuguese between 6th April 1737, when the war began, and the 13th February 1740, amounted to nearly the whole of the Northern Provinces, 22 leagues in length, viz., from Versevá to Damão, with their four chief ports and 340 villages, and a revenue of over 20,000 cruzados.* They lost, besides Baçaim, eight cities, 20 fortresses, two fortified hills, the famous island of Salsette, where was situated the fortress of Taná and the city of the same name, the Ilha das Vaccas, and that of Juem, called Caranja Island. Damão escaped, as did also Chaul and Dio. In Goa they had lost Salsette. On the Goanese continent Bardez was also lost. The Government of the Viceroy was thus reduced to the Island of Goa, which is two leagues long (from Nossa Senhora do Cabo to S. Thyago) and nearly six in circumference, Chorão, Piedale, S. Estevão, and Combarjua, and the Island of Angediva, nine leagues south of Marmagão, a very small island, simply held to prevent any pirates settling there.

The losses at sea were also very heavy, and of the greatest consequence to the State, whose vessels had formerly been always respected and feared by the enemy.

The value of the implements of war, ammunition, &c., lost in the various fortresses, cities, and ships, exceeded 2,000,000 cruzados,† exclusive of 593 pieces of artillery, several being of bronze and of large calibre.

---

*2,500*l*. † 250,000*l*.

The expenses during two years of the war amounted to 3,440,000 xerafins,* an almost incredible amount considering the small number of troops engaged.

Such was the state of affairs when Dom Luiz de Menezes, Conde da Ericeira, arrived in India as Viceroy, on the 13th May 1741. He was accompanied by a strong reinforcement of European troops, with which he inflicted a signal defeat on the Mahrattas in Bardez, capturing the forts of Sanguem and Supem, and retaking the fort of Ponda. Shortly before his arrival in India the Bounsulo had invaded Bardez, and Angria had been attacking the Portuguese by sea; the resources of the Government were in such straits that, in order to save Goa, it had been deemed necessary to hand over Chaul to the Mahrattas. The Treaty under which this last-named concession was made, is dated the 18th September 1740, and contained the following stipulations:—

Tratados, T. VI., p. 202.

The Balagi Bagi Rao Pardane agreed to withdraw his troops from Salsette and Bardez, and to deliver the fort of Coculim to the Portuguese in the same condition in which it was when captured; the city of Damão and the fort of S. Hieronimo were to be retained by the Portuguese, who were to receive also from the Bagi Rao the Pergunnah Naer; the Portuguese agreed not to interfere with the jurisdiction of Baçaim, Damão, Salsette, Bellaflor, Caranjá, Chaul, and Morro; nor to molest the territories of Salsette, Bardez, or Pergunnah Naer, nor to concern themselves with the districts of Ponda, Zambaulim, Panebamal, Saundem, and Bidnur; they further agreed to assist the Bagi Rao with their fleets, should the latter be at war with the Angria; and to deliver up the city of Chaul, with all its artillery and ammunition. The gates of Chaul were to be guarded by British† troops until advices should

* About 230,000*l.*

† Negotiations for this Treaty were carried out for the Portuguese

be received that the people of the Bagi Rao had retired from Salsette and Bardez.

During the governorship of the Marquez de Castello Novo e Alorna, which extended from 1744 to 1750, the Portuguese arms, under his command, captured the forts of Tiracol, Sanquelim, Bicholim, and Neutim; but in 1754 the last-named place, as well as Rarim, was handed back to the Bounsulo, as they had previously formed part of his territory.

Tratados, T. VII., p. 15.

The Treaty under which the transfer of these places was effected is dated the 25th October. It commences by a stipulation that missionaries are to have full liberty to carry on their labours in the territories of the Bounsulo, and that the Dessayes* of Query, Sanquelim, Morly, and others who may have sworn fealty to the State of Portugal, shall be protected by His most Faithful Majesty. It then goes on to declare that the Sar Dessayes of Pergunnah Cudalle shall at once cede all rights to Alorna, Bicholim, the province of Pernem, and the castles of Morly and Saterem, as also the fort of Tiracol, to the Portuguese, whilst the latter are to cede to the Dessayes the cities of Rarim and Neutim. The Dessayes' vessels are not to seize or molest vessels trading to Portuguese ports. As the Dessayes are not in a position to pay for damage done by them to Portuguese shipping during previous wars, or the tribute money owing since 1739, those debts are to be cancelled, but tribute is to be payable from the date of publication of this Treaty. The Sar Dessaye (the Bounsulo) finally promises, on behalf of himself, of his son, and of his heirs, not to disturb the Portuguese, nor to give any assistance to their enemies.

---

by Captain James Inchbird, under instructions from the Governor of Bombay, Mr. Stephen Law. Full details of these transactions are contained in the Bombay Consultations for the year 1740.

* The Dessaye was a native official in principal revenue charge of a district, often held hereditarily. Sometimes also a petty chief.

Shortly after this (at the end of February 1756) a body of Mahrattas invaded Sunda, under the pretext that certain tributes were in arrear. The King of Sunda, not being able to pay, offered to give as security any fortress in his dominions which the Mahratta Chief might choose, upon which he selected Ponda, with a view to its proximity to Goa. Seeing this, the Viceroy resolved to march an army against him. He accordingly set out in April with a force, and took up a position on the top of a hill, from whence he commenced to bombard Ponda. The troops, without waiting for the word of command, seeing some damage effected on the enemy's works, rushed forward to the assault, when they were repulsed with great slaughter. On this the Viceroy ordered those that were with him to support the others, he placing himself at their head, but they were again entirely routed and the Viceroy killed (this happened on the 28th June), whereupon the army retired to Goa.

Evora, Cod. CXVI., 2—11, No. 26.

Four years after signing the Treaty above referred to, the Bounsulo, on the 9th April 1758, declared war against the Portuguese on account of the oppression of the people by taxes, and of their being obliged to buy tobacco at Goa; but, more particularly, it was thought, because, owing to the declining power of the Portuguese, he considered it a good opportunity to regain the fortresses of Tiracol, Alorna, and Bicholim. Pernem and Sanquelim were captured by the Bounsulo, but his troops were forced to retire from before the three fortresses above referred to. Had these places fallen, it was feared that the Bounsulo would have been joined by the Mahrattas. The Viceroy now determined to carry the war into the enemy's country, and he accordingly took up a position on the hill Ammona, which he fortified, thus placing himself between the Bounsulo and the Mahrattas, so as

Conselho Ultramarinho, Maço 57, Nos. 4, 5, and 37.

to prevent communications between them. The enemy retired to three neighbouring pagodas, where the Portuguese attacked them and forced them to fall back on Sanquelim. Shortly after this the Bounsulo sent to ask for a peace.

The Mahrattas were now at war with the King of Sunda, who sent to the Viceroy for assistance, but the latter was unable to render any aid beyond supplying him with some powder; and he only did this in the hope of eventually getting back the province of Ponda, which had formerly belonged to Sunda.

Tratados, T. VII., p. 111.

On the 26th July 1759 a secret treaty was concluded with the Bounsulo, in which the Viceroy undertook to recommend the King of Portugal to restore to him all, or a portion of, the provinces which he, the Bounsulo, ceded to the State under the Treaty of the 25th October 1754 (*vide* p. 100).

Conselho Ultramarinho, Maço 57, No. 37.

On the 26th October 1760, the Viceroy entered into a treaty with Balagi Bagi Rao, surnamed the Nana, in which the latter undertook to hand over to the Viceroy the provinces of Zambaulin, Supem, Sanguem, and Ponda, in order that the latter might restore them to the King of Sunda, in consideration of which the Viceroy pledged himself to send a fleet with 500 Portuguese soldiers to capture the fortresses of Zanzira* and Canssa, which he would then hand over to the Nana, and the latter thereupon bound himself to pay 100,000 rupees each year to the King of Portugal, secured upon the tribute payable by the King of Sunda. At the close of the enterprise the Nana bound himself to give an additional 50,000 rupees to the Portuguese troops. When, in accordance with this agreement, the Portuguese fleet,

Conselho Ultramarinho, Maço 57, No. 34.

* Janjira, 44 miles south of Bombay, and Kansa Island and fort about two miles from it, off the district of Nandgaon.

which went to assist the Mahrattas, arrived off Rajapur, on the 21st February 1761, they found the British flag flying over the two fortresses of Zanzira and Canssa, and an English fleet in the harbour. Wind failing, the Portuguese vessels cast anchor outside the harbour, and they were there visited by a British naval officer who proved to them, by documentary evidence, that the fortresses had already been surrendered by the Sidy to the English.*

---

* Extract from a Letter from the Governor and Council of Bombay, dated 4th April 1761 :—

"128. The Sciddee of Gingerah, forced by the distress that place was in, came here in a private manner on the 1st December, notwithstanding the strict injunction we laid on him last season, and we finding, from the succours sent the Morattas from Goa, that it must fall into their hands without we assisted him, we resolved in consultation the 9th December to supply him with provisions, stores, and some ready money, altogether amounting to twenty thousand (20,000) rupees, but in such manner as not to give umbrage to the Morattas. On the 12th of that month the President laid before us the Sciddee's mortgage bond of his houses, &c., at Surat, and revenues under Gingerah to your Honours for the supplies we had and might afford him, and on the 24th February he likewise presented translate of a letter from the Sciddee, setting forth that the Portuguese were sending further succours to the Morattas, offering to deliver Gingerah and Consaw to your Honours, and declaring, if we did not accept it, he would invite the Dutch or some other Europeans to support him, and we, considering that the Portuguese might probably seize upon the place for themselves, and that the President last year told Govin Seurum Punt, we would not allow it to fall into improper hands. We appointed Mr. Byfeld, Major Gouin, and Mr. Hornby, a committee to proceed to Gingerah with your Honours' ships "Neptune," "Guardian," "Fox Ketch," "Syren Snow," "Dolphin," "Shark," "Bonetta," and "Otter Gallivats," with proper detachments of military to confer with Ramajee Punt, assuring him that our design in sending those gentlemen was only to interpose as mediators between the Sciddee and Nannah to accommodate their differences, in an amicable manner, but that if, notwithstanding the Committee's endeavours for that purpose, Ramajee Punt would not withdraw his forces, they should acquaint him we were determined to hoist the British colours both at Gingerah and Consaw till their differences might be properly adjusted. The Committee set out the 2nd ultimo, and under No. 62 is copy of our instructions to them, wherein your Honours will perceive the place is assigned over to you, and that the President wrote a suitable letter to Ramajee Punt also that we were in hopes he would be induced to raise the siege imme-

Early in 1763, the Mahrattas having captured a Portuguese vessel coming from Macao, the Viceroy induced the King of Sunda

Conselho Ultramarinho, Maço 57, No. 5.

---

diately, in which case we instructed the Committee to return, after leaving such a detachment as the Major might think proper, and getting the principal Sciddees to join with their Master in signing an obligation that they would never permit any Europeans but the English to settle or carry on any trade there, or in any other part of their dominions, which was immediately consented to, and the Committee, soon after their arrival, having certain intelligence that the Portuguese fleet were in the neighbourhood, consisting of a frigate, a small galley, a sloop, and Munchuas having four hundred (400) Europeans and Mustees, and two hundred (200) Coffrees on board, hoisted our colours at Gingerah and Consaw, and Ramajee Punt declaring afterwards that, unless the two principal Sciddees were brought to Bombay and the forts of Gingerah and Consaw garrisoned by our people, he would not withdraw his forces, and Ramajee Punt Bawa, who it was said was sent by Nannah to supersede him in the command of the army, being averse to it without an absolute order from Poonah, We, on the 10th ultimo, took into consideration the Committee obliging the Morattas to retire without reach of the guns from Gingerah and Consaw, but, as Ramajee Punt Bawa alleged that he waited for orders from Poonah, we directed them to declare that, in consideration of that circumstance, if he did not withdraw his forces by the 25th ultimo, we should consider it as an insult to our colours. The President at the same time despatched a letter to the Regency at Poonah, desiring that orders might be immediately sent Ramajee, through our Agent there, to be delivered Ramajee by the Committee for withdrawing his forces, declaring that we should put the above construction on their refusal. The Committee having acquainted us that one of the redoubts opposite to Gingerah Fort, and within gunshot, was garrisoned by Portuguese sent from Goa, tho' our colours were hoisted there, and deeming it very inconsistent, as we are not at war with that nation, we ordered the Committee to inquire of the commanding officer the reasons of it, and to acquaint him that, if he did not immediately withdraw his men, they should treat him as an enemy, and, provided he declined retiring in a reasonable time, to oblige him, making Ramajee previously sensible of our resolution; however that garrison withdrew without the Committee being obliged to go those lengths.

"129. On the 9th ultimo, the Portuguese appearing in sight, the Committee ordered Captain Purling to stop up the port of Gingerah, tho' on their writing a suitable letter to the commanding officer not to interfere as the place was assigned over to your Honours, he assured them he should return to Goa with the troops, as he should always endeavour to preserve the friendship subsisting between the two Crowns."

and the Bounsulo to assist him in punishing them. The King of Sunda promised to send 10,000 men, whilst the Bounsulo was to remain neutral; and as it had been discovered that some of the Mahratta Chiefs were disposed to rise against their Sovereign, a combination was made, and all agreed to meet on a certain day to march together against Mandangor. The King of Sunda failed, however, to keep his engagement, and only one of the rebel chieftains appeared, with 70 men, the others all remaining neutral. The Viceroy thereupon resolved to act by himself, and to besiege the fortress with his own troops alone. After a siege of 14 days, the commander of Mandangor capitulated on the last day of May 1763, when his troops were allowed to march out with their arms, and the Portuguese took possession of the place, which up to that time had been considered impregnable. The fortress was immediately demolished, and the district annexed to the Portuguese possessions. It was subsequently, by treaty, annexed to Sunda, but garrisoned by a Portuguese force in the pay of the King of Sunda.

Conselho Ultramarinho, No. 11; Tratados, T. VIII, p. 62.

On the 17th December 1779, a treaty of peace was concluded between the Portuguese and the Peishwa Madou Rao, in accordance with which the fleets of the two parties were not to attack one another at sea, but to provide each other with any necessaries they might require, and to trade freely in their respective ports. All disagreements between them were to be settled by arbitration, and whilst the Portuguese bound themselves not to render assistance to the enemies of the Peishwa, the latter agreed not to help the enemies of Portugal. The Portuguese were not to erect forts at Guzerat, Sant, Cantevad, Surat, or other places belonging to Madou Rao. In consideration of the existing friendship between the two parties, the Peishwa agreed to hand over to the Portuguese certain villages in Damão, of the annual value of 12,000 rupees, on condition that no forts were to be erected in them.

Conselho Ultramarinho, No. 37.

In 1785 the Mahrattas sent an embassy to Goa to propose that the Portuguese forces should join with those of the Mahrattas and the Bounsulo, to make war on the Nabob. This, however, the Viceroy declined to do, believing that it was a blind on the part of the Mahrattas to get possession of Bicholim and Punem; he therefore marched troops to the frontier for the defence of those parts.

Conselho Ultramarinho, No. 93.

At this place it may not be inappropriate to give a brief review of the position of the Portuguese territories in India in the latter years of the eighteenth century. Writing on the 4th February 1780, the Viceroy, Dom Frederico Guilherme de Sousa reported that, on his arrival in India in the preceding year, he found Goa in a most deplorable condition; entire streets were without houses, and others in which there existed only ruins. The old houses were all falling into decay, whilst their landlords were not in a position to repair them. Of its old magnificence nothing remained but the Cathedral and the Convents. Goa had then 87 old and small houses; some had floors, whilst others were on the ground, and nine were unfinished. Amongst the palm groves were 350 huts, roofed with palm leaves, in which resided the renters of the palm trees, tavern keepers, Caffres, Mulattos, and other poor people. The Senate of Goa, in the preceding year, had 39,493 xerafins receipts and expenses 38,252 xerafins. The number of convents in Goa was ten, in which were 63 nuns, and their revenues amounted to 39,216 xerafins. The commerce of Goa was on the decline because the business of the Natives depended almost entirely upon the goods sent out from Portugal, as they were too much wanting in energy to seek after other sources of trade. The local produce consisted then chiefly of cocoa, areca, salt, and spirits, which were sent to the ports to the north and south in small vessels. The expenses of the Royal Treasury exceeded the receipts by 200,000 xerafins, whilst the receipts of the Camara were scarcely sufficient to meet the necessary expenses. The inhabitants, reduced to poverty and misery, had no means of improving their positions by increasing their commerce. "Thus," the Viceroy remarked, "unless the necessary means be applied for "re-establishing trade, the place must inevitably soon "be entirely ruined."

Conselho Ultramarinho, No. 60.

The Bounsulo having failed for eight years to pay to the Portuguese Crown his annual tribute of 4,000 xerafins, and having made continual piratical attacks on Portuguese merchant vessels, and usurped the rents of the Dessayes, vassals of the King of Portugal, the Viceroy captured from him, by surprise, the fortress of Bicholim, on the 25th August 1781. On the following day he took the strong house of Sanquelim, and annexed the territories subject to their respective jurisdictions. On the 1st October 1782 the Bounsulo collected troops and occupied the village of Gululem, in Bicholim, and the following day he occupied also the villages of Dumachem and Salem. A Portuguese force was immediately despatched against him. Several skirmishes took place in different villages, with loss to the enemy, who, however, had also entered with a large force into Bardez, burning everything as they went along. On the 22nd the opposing forces met on the bank of the Macazana river, in Bardez, where an engagement took place, which appears to have been indecisive. The Portuguese followed up the Bounsulo's forces and inflicted upon them several defeats. Reinforcements having been received by the enemy the Portuguese General retired. The troops of the Bounsulo continued to advance, and many of the people of the villages which they burnt fled to the Island of Goa for protection. On the 24th November, the enemy attacked the fort of Sanquelim. Reinforcements were sent up, which arrived on the 7th December, and these immediately attacked the enemy, who after a fight of 2¼ hours were put to flight and their baggage was all captured. After throwing reinforcements into Sanquelim, the Portuguese returned to Bicholim, whence a force was sent to guard the frontier of Bardez, which was threatened by the enemy, and the fortresses of Marmagão, Agoada, and Rachol were garrisoned by auxiliaries. On the 18th January 1783, the Bounsulo appeared before the fort of Bicholim with 4,000 infantry and some cavalry. On the 6th February he attacked the fort of Querim, but was repulsed with loss. On the 23rd March, a force of 3,726 Portuguese left Bardez and went against the enemy, whom they dislodged from a neighbouring hill; they then marched against the Bounsulo's camp, near Manacurem, in Bicholim, where he had fortified himself on the summit of a hill, which was speedily captured from the enemy who, apparently, offered no resistance. The Portuguese then encamped at Alorna, occupying both sides of the river. The main force of the enemy was attacked at Manerim, and totally defeated. The villages of Alorna, Vaidangor, and other places were then annexed and garrisoned by the Portuguese, whereupon the Bounsulo sued for peace, which was granted.

Conselho Ultramarinho, No. 28.

In a letter of the 2nd January 1781, the Viceroy stated to the King that the English had supplied arms and munitions of war to the Mahrattas which enabled them to capture the Island of Salsette, Bardez, and Chaul, by which the principal houses in Goa had been reduced to great poverty. The reputation of the Army of India had also been ruined thereby, as well as the Portuguese trade with that country. Hearing that the English contemplated an alliance with Ragoba, for the conquest from the Mahrattas of Baçaim, Chaul, and other villages of the ancient jurisdiction of Damão, the Viceroy sent a protest to the Council at Bombay, wherein he stated that the forts, &c., of the East Indies, extending from Chaul to Damão had, for two hundred years, belonged to the Crown of Portugal; that although the Mahrattas had captured several of those places nearly forty years ago, the Crown of Portugal refused to surrender its claim to the same, or its right to recover them on the occurrence of a suitable opportunity. It was claimed that, in the gift of the Island of Bombay to the English, it had been stipulated that the British Crown should in no case interfere with the Portuguese jurisdiction over the other islands of Baçaim, or its land, nor deprive the State of India of its commerce and liberty; but that by the Treaty of Peace, the English were bound to assist the Portuguese on every occasion they might require aid with the view of recovering their former possessions in the North. The Viceroy accordingly emphatically called upon the Council at Bombay to desist from this enterprise.

The Council of Bombay, in reply, stated that the Island of Salsette had been captured by the English troops in 1774, and their reasons for so doing had been fully explained in reply to the protest made, at the time, by the Governor of that place; that being involved in a war with the Mahrattas, they would attack his forces wherever they might be; that the places referred to had been in the Mahrattas' possession for nearly half a century; and that in an assault upon any fort where their flag might be flying they could not stay to consult history before the batteries were opened to ascertain the ancient possessors of these places, or consider whether they would attempt their reconquest at some future period. The Portuguese, the Council remarked, acquired their possessions in India by right of conquest, and having now lost those of the North, their right to them had ceased in the same manner as it had originated. With regard to the obligations of the English towards the Portuguese, as laid down in the treaty of cession of the Island of Bombay, the Council remarked that it was to assist and protect them in their traffic and navigation, and that it was clearly defined, in a secret treaty made at the same time, that this assistance was limited to their protection against the Dutch, with whom the Portuguese were then at enmity, and that the Articles quoted in no way referred to their ancient possessions in the North. Accordingly the Council expressed themselves unable to accept the protest of the Portuguese Viceroy, and they repudiated all responsibility for any consequences that might result from such measures as might be taken thereon by the Crown of Portugal.

Conselho Ultramarinho, No. 33.

On the plea that the King of Sunda had violated the terms of a Treaty of 1742, an expeditionary force was sent against him in 1752, when the forts of Piro, Chunpun, and others were captured and held as hostages far the due fulfilment of his obligations. The King having been subsequently attacked by the Mahrattas in 1763, the Portuguese went to his assistance and expelled the invaders, whereupon they occupied his provinces, and he retired to Portuguese territory receiving from them a pension of 23,000 xerafins. In 1790 the King of Sunda, then under the protection of the Portuguese, expressed a desire to send an emissary to the Mahrattas with the view of regaining his kingdom, offering, should he be successful, to remain a vassal of the Crown of Portugal, and to allow Portuguese troops to garrison any forts that might be recaptured. The Viceroy, however, very much discouraged this proposal, being apprehensive that the King of Sunda would take the opportunity of throwing himself into the hands of the Mahrattas or of the

English, and he took every opportunity to prevent such an occurrence. Whilst deliberations on the subject were proceeding, news reached the Viceroy that a fleet had been seen in the vicinity of Piro, but it was uncertain whether it belonged to the Mahrattas or to the English. This event expedited matters, and a treaty was concluded with the King of Sunda on the 17th January 1791, in which the latter abdicated to the Crown of Portugal all his rights in the territories of Ponda, Zambaulim, and Panchama, with their dependencies, as well as the fortress of Cabo da Rama and the jurisdiction of Canacona. He also agreed to certain allowances for the support of a Portuguese garrison for Piro. It being alleged by the King of Sunda that Dom José I., the late King of Portugal, had promised his father to restore to him the Provinces of Ponda and Zambaulim, as soon as he should be in a position to hold them, it was agreed, in a Secret Clause of the abovementioned Treaty, that the Governor and Captain General should lay the matter before the Queen of Portugal with the view of that promise being now carried out.

Tratados, T. IX., p. 4.

In consequence of this treaty, a force was despatched to Rachol on the 18th January, and having collected reinforcements at that place, the Portuguese General appeared before Piro when he found it in the possession of the Mahrattas, whose fleet also commanded it by sea. Within the fort, however, were many troops favourable to the King of Sunda, with whom the Portuguese General managed to communicate, with the result that eventually, on the 30th January, his troops were admitted without hostility. In March following, the Mahrattas called upon the Portuguese to deliver up Piro to them, but they managed, by diplomacy, to avoid doing so.

PORTUGUESE INDIA.

SECTION V.

THE RED SEA AND PERSIAN GULF.

The first Portuguese subjects to visit Ormuz were probably Rabbi Abraham of Beja and Joseph of Lamego; the former subsequently accompanied Pedro de Covilham to that island and to Aden, full particulars of which places were sent home to King John II.

At a very early date the Portuguese recognized the necessity of stopping the trade of the Moors with India, with the view of monopolising it themselves, and accordingly, in 1503, Antonio de Saldanha was sent from Lisbon with a fleet, to cruise off the mouth of the Red Sea against the ships of Mecca. This interference with the trade which used to pass through Egypt seriously affected the revenues of the Soldan of Cairo, and he, in retaliation for the losses he suffered in consequence, threatened to destroy the Temple and Holy Places of Jerusalem.

In 1506* the King sent out a fleet from Lisbon, under the command of Tristão da Cunha, and with him was Affonso de Albuquerque who was to cruize with a part of the fleet off the coast of Arabia. After the capture of several places on the east coast of Africa, the combined fleets took the Island of Socotra. Leaving there on the 20th August 1507, Tristão de Cunha proceeded to India, whilst Affonso de Albuquerque† went towards Ormuz

* Faria-y-Souza, T. 1, pt. II., cap. 1; Lendas da India, T. 1, p. 658.

† Unfortunately the letters from Affonso de Albuquerque giving accounts of his attacks on the towns in Arabia and on Ormuz on this occasion are not now in existence.

which was his ultimate destination. On his way thither he entirely destroyed Calayate and Curiate, and having burned Muscat he proceeded to Soar, where he concluded a Treaty with the natives, who became vassals of the King of Portugal. Albuquerque then, after destroying Orfação, proceeded to Ormuz where he met with some opposition, but, having defeated the Royal troops with heavy loss, he forced the King to sign a treaty the conditions of which were:

That the King of Ormuz should be restored to his Kingdom of which he had been dispossessed by force of arms;

Tratados, T. I., p. 1.

that the King should become a vassal of the King of Portugal, and pay an annual tribute of 20,000 xerafins* in

Cartas, p. 16.

gold and a further sum down of 5,000 xerafins towards the expenses of the war; also that the King should hand over a place, outside the town, for the erection of a fortress and factory. The date of this Treaty was September 1507.

Albuquerque immediately proceeded to erect a fort at Ormuz, and opened a house for trade within the town. He

Cartas, p. 100.

then departed, and, in a letter of the 8th November 1512, he advised the King not to give up the contract and agreement with Ormuz, remarking that 30,000 xerafins of tribute would be nothing for that place to pay. The great thing wanted there was, he said, a fortress and factory, which would enable the Portuguese to see the grand† place it was. The people there, he added, knew

---

* About 1,400*l.* a year. In a letter to the King of 6th February 1508 Albuquerque assured His Majesty that he came to no terms with the people of Ormuz, but after having thoroughly defeated them he handed the place over to the King for him to govern it in the name of the King, D. Manoel of Portugal, and charged him with an annual tribute of 15,000 xerafins in gold.

† Abd-er-Razzák, who visited Ormuz in 1442, remarked of it "Ormuz, which is also called Djerrun, is a port situated in the middle of the sea, and which has not its equal on the surface of the globe. The

the value of the place and kept it secret, being aware that, if once taken, it would be always held.

Having subsequently succeeded as Viceroy of India, Albuquerque fitted out a fleet of twenty vessels which he commanded in person, and which sailed from Goa on the 8th February 1513 for the capture of Aden. Aden was unsuccessfully attacked on the morning of the 27th March, and Albuquerque thereupon sailed for the Red Sea.* Here he conceived a project for diverting the waters of the Nile, by means of a canal, so as to destroy the trade of Cairo; and he also contemplated an expedition of four hundred horsemen, which he proposed should be disembarked in the harbour of Yembo, whence they should march direct to the temple of Medina, which was to be stripped of all its treasures, and the body of Mahomet was to be carried away with the view of ransoming the Temple of Jerusalem in exchange for it. It is needless to remark that neither of these projects was put into effect. On his return from the Red Sea he again bombarded Aden and then proceeded to Goa, whence he wrote to the King, under date the 20th October 1514, stating that a fort at Aden was necessary. The

Cartas, p. 279.

merchants of seven climates from Egypt, Syria, the country of Roum (Anatolia), Azerbijan, Irak-Arabi, and Irak-Adjemi, the provinces of Fars, Khorassan, Ma-wara-amahar, Turkistan, the kingdom of Deschti-Kaptchack (in Tartary), the countries inhabited by the Kalmucks, the whole of the kingdoms of Tchin (China) and Matchin (Southern China), and the city of Khanbálik (Pekin) all make their way to this port; the inhabitants of the sea coasts arrive here from the countries of Tchin, Java, Bengal, the cities of Zirbad, Tenasserim, Sokotora, Schahrinou, the islands of Dîwah-Mahall (the Maldives), the countries of Malabar, Abyssinia, Zanguebar, the ports of Bidjanagar, Kalbergah, Gudjarat, Kanbait (Cambay), the coasts of Arabia, which extend as far as Aden, Jiddah, and Yembo; they bring hither those rare and precious articles which the sun, the moon, and the rains have combined to bring to perfection, and which are capable of being transported by sea. Travellers from all countries resort hither, and, in exchange for the commodities they bring, they can without trouble or difficulty obtain all that they desire." ("India in the Fifteenth Century."—*Hakluyt Society*).

* This was the first Portuguese fleet that entered the Red Sea.

existing port, he said, was a good one, where the Portuguese ships could winter. A force of 4,000 would, he considered, be sufficient to take the place, and if the Island of Cirna were captured, Aden would at once fall.

Cartas, p. 326.

In a letter dated five days later, he informed the King that he had determined to go again to the Red Sea and take Meçua (Macowa Island), Dalaca (Dhalac Archipelago), and Juda (Jidda, near Mecca).

In 1521 a Portuguese fleet* sailed up the Persian Gulf as far as Bahrein, and captured that place for the King of Ormuz, as it had revolted against him. Bahrein revolted again in 1529, but upon the reappearance of the Portuguese fleet it again submitted. Acting on the advice of his officers, the captain of the fleet attempted to take the place, but he was defeated.

Tratados, T. I., p. 40.

A new treaty was concluded by the Governor Dom Duarte de Menezes and the King of Ormuz, on the 15th July 1523, in accordance with the terms of which the King of Ormuz was to give to Portugal houses in a safe and convenient place for the use of its merchants; Portuguese ships were to be exempt from duties, and Portugal was to defend Ormuz against all enemies; Ormuz ships were to have perfect freedom to navigate anywhere excepting in the Straits of Mecca, and the coasts about Sofala; all the Moors were forbidden to carry arms, and all the arms in the King's arsenal were to be given up and placed in the Portuguese fort. In January 1524 Heytor da Silveira sailed from Goa with a fleet for Aden, and concluded a treaty with the King of that place, in accordance with which a gold crown worth 2,000 xerafins was to be annually presented to the King of Portugal, and Aden was to be a free port to all vessels. This treaty was, however, not adhered to. Subsequently,

* Lendas da India, T. II., p. 647.

in 1530, a new treaty was concluded under which the King of Aden became a vassal* of the King of Portugal, and agreed to a tribute of 10,000 pardaos in gold annually, of which he was to pay down at once the sum of 1,500 pardaos, with which to make, in Ormuz, a gold crown for the King of Portugal. The King of Aden's ships were to be at liberty to navigate with perfect freedom where they liked, with the exception of Mecca.

MSS., Vol. A., 2, 28.

In 1543 the King of Ormuz handed the Portuguese the Customs receipts, amounting to 300,000 cruzados, in satisfaction of the many thousand xerafins which he then owed as tribute.

In 1546 the Turks sent a fleet to oppose the power of Portugal in the Persian Gulf. Their first attack was on Kesheen and Dhofar, which places they destroyed; they then proceeded to Muscat† and bombarded the town, without doing much damage, but sailed away again without venturing to land their men. The following year‡ Dom Payo de Noronha, with three small ships, visited Aden, where he was well received, and the Moor, Soleyman Bacha, (who had hanged the King), gave up the city and fortress to him, wishing to become a vassal of Portugal on condition of receiving assistance against the Rumes (Turks). De Noronha sent to Goa for reinforcements, but, before these arrived, the Turks came one night in such numbers that the Portuguese left the fortress and retired to their ships. The Turks, on hearing that the Portuguese had left the city, captured it with the greatest ease, and drove Soleyman inland. A few years later the Turks returned to the attack of Muscat, a detailed account of which event is given in a letter

Gav. 1, M. 89, D. 7.

from Reys Nordin, Guazil at Ormuz, to the King of Portugal, dated 25th October 1552. From this it appears

---

* De Barros, T. IV., pt. 1, p. 422.
† Lendas da India, T. IV., p. 525.
‡ Lendas da India, T. IV., p. 627.

that a Turkish fleet of 19 ships, commanded by Mamede Beque and Pire Beque, the latter of whom had recently taken Aden from the Arabs, appeared off that port about the 15th August 1552, and remained there inactive for six days. The Turks then began to attack the place and bombarded it for two days, during which the besieged suffered hardly any loss. Notwithstanding this, the garrison capitulated on the morning of the third day on condition that they should be allowed to go free to Ormuz. The Turks, however, took all the garrison, loaded them with chains, and set them to row in their gallies. There appears to have been some treachery in the surrender of the town, but João de Lisboa, who was captain there, blamed his troops on this account, whilst they laid all the responsibility on him. The Turks did not retain Muscat, but, after spoiling it and removing all the guns from the fort, they retired and proceeded to the attack of Ormuz, arriving off that place on the 19th September. Having landed a force,* they erected batteries, and bombarded the fort for a whole month, but without inflicting so much damage as they received. After plundering the city the Turks retired as they had done at Muscat.

Muscat† was again occupied by the Portuguese after the retirement of Pire Beque; but in 1580 Meer Ali Beg attacked the town by land and sea, and, having defeated the Portuguese garrison, sacked the place, and then retired with his booty.

MSS., Vol. A., 2, 28.
D.R., Vol. 45, fol. 326, vo.

By order of the Governor, Manoel de Sousa Coutinho, a fortress was founded at Muscat in the year 1588; and in the following year the Princes of Muscat, upon the death of their father, made over to the King of Portugal half the revenues of the

---

* Faria-y-Sousa, T. 2, p. 164.

† Selections from Government of India Records, No. CCVII.

Bandel of Muscat towards the building of the fortress. About the same time, in obedience to orders from Madrid, a fort was also erected at Soar.

The appearance of Robert Shirley in Persia was the cause of great anxiety to the Portuguese, who give the following account* of him and his mission:—

"In this decade there appears an Englishman named Robert Shirley, who, having been sent to Spain by the Shah of Persia in 1603, sometimes appears as an Ambassador, sometimes as a merchant. After a residence of some years at Madrid he suddenly disappeared, having left for England, where he revealed to the British Government the object of his visit to Spain. In the beginning of November 1613, a letter from Philip III. warned the authorities in India that Robert Shirley had negotiated in England vessels with which to attack Ormuz, and that he had started from Europe armed with powers to conclude a treaty with the Shah for commerce in silk goods. The Spanish King insisted that Ormuz should be fortified against the English, and requested that all means should be employed for the capture of the Ambassador to the King of Persia. Every effort to that effect, however, failed, although the officer charged with this matter, Dom Louis da Gama, was a most intelligent man. Robert Shirley managed to escape him and passed into Persia, where he plotted and brought about the great calamities which, after the arrival of the English, overtook the Portuguese possessions in Asia."

News reached Goa in January 1617 that the British contemplated the erection of a fort at Jasque,† and it

---

* Decade XIII., by Antonio Bocarro, p. 9.

† Decade XIII., by Antonio Bocarro, p. 672. That there was some ground for this supposition is proved by letters from Mr. Connock, East India Company's Agent at Ispahan, who, writing to the Court (19th January 1617), pointing out that Jask was a fit place for fortification, "which," he added, "I doubt not but from the Sophy to obtain." Later on (4th August) he wrote, describing an interview with the King of Persia, on which occasion His Majesty called for wine, and in a large bowl drank His Majesty's (of England) health upon his knee, saying that Connock was welcome, that the King of England should be his elder brother, that "his friendship he did dearly esteem and tender, that he "would grant us Jask or any other port we would require, and such "freedom in every respect as in his honour he might grant, and all this "in the Spanish Agent's presence, to whom he hath neither offered good "word nor countenance from that to this hour, but hath graced me "with four several presents."—O. C., Vol. IV., 436; Vol. V., 519.

was this fact, coupled with orders from Portugal that the English were to be prevented from trading with Persia, that led to the engagement* with British ships off that port, which ended in the defeat of the Portuguese fleet that was sent there to oppose them.

The engagement off Jask was ere long followed by an attack on Ormuz by the combined forces of the Persians and English, which resulted in the capture of the city on the 10th February, and the surrender of the castle to the English on the 23rd April 1622. In this engagement Ruy Frere's fleet† was destroyed by the English without any action on his part to prevent it. He himself was taken prisoner and carried to Surat, where he managed to escape,‡ and having obtained a

---

* Two engagements were fought between the fleets on the 17th and 28th December 1620 respectively, on each of which occasions the Portuguese fleet, which was commanded by Ruy Frere Andrade, retired "with dishonour." During the second engagement Captain Andrew Shilling, who commanded the English fleet, was struck by a shot in the shoulder, from the effects of which he died on the 6th January 1621. —W. Pinder, Master of the E. I. Co.'s Ship "London."—"Purchas Pilgrimes," Vol. 2, p. 1788.

† Mr. Edward Monox, the Company's Agent in Persia, gives the following account of this event: "The nineteenth January (1622) we "set sayle towards Ormuz, where we arrived the two-and-twentieth, and "that night anchored in front of the towne, about two leagues from the "Castle, in expectation that the enemy's Armada, consisting of five "galeons and some fifteen or twenty frigats, would have come forth to "fight us, but they hailed so near the Castle that we could not come at "them, which we perceiving, and understanding that our vowed enemie, "Ruy Frere, was in his new erected Castle of Kishme, the next day we "addressed ourselves towards the said Castle, where wo arrived in fit "time to save both the lives and reputation of the Portugals, not able "long to hold out against the Persian siege, and willing rather to yield "to us. The first of February they yielded both their persons and "Castle, after many meetings and treaties, into our possession."—O. C., Vol. VIII., 1032. Printed in "Purchas Pilgrimes," Vol. 2, p. 1793.

‡ Ruy Frere was sent to Surat on board the "Lion," and the account of his escape thence is thus given in a letter from that place of the 11th May 1622: "That which most discredits us hath been the reccles "negligence of (the) Master and people of the 'Lion,' who, notwith-

vessel he returned to Ormuz, which place having already fallen he went on to Muscat.

D.R., Livro 17, fols. 178, 213.

At the trial of the several officers concerned in the loss of Ormuz, Ruy Frere was exonerated from all blame principally, it would seem, because his services were required in the Persian Gulf, where his name was a terror to the Arabs. Ruy Frere died in 1633. Dom Gonsalvo da Sylveira, Captain-Mor of the galleys, attributed his not fighting the enemy to his Captains having refused to assist him; one of these was Louis de Brito de Vasconçellos, who, after a trial which lasted some months, was condemned to eight years' transportation to Trinquimale; but in 1643 that sentence was quashed. Simão de Mello, Captain of the Fort, was however condemned to death, but as he had escaped to the land of the Moors his sentence was carried out in effigy. In 1631, instructions were sent out to the Viceroy that he should endeavour to come to terms with the Governor of Ormuz, even to buying the place of him if necessary.

D. R., Livro 33, fol. 13.

D. R., Livro 46, fol. 91.

D. R., Livro 48, fol. 140.

D. R., Livro 28, fol. 87.

" standing our often and exp(ress) charge, as well per wrighting as per " word of mouth, to continue a str(ict) gard on Ruy Ffrere's person, and " constantly to releave the same (by) turnes, to prevent whatsoever his " intents, either escape or otherwise, they suffered both him and three " more of his company with a skife in the night to worke their owne " libertie."—O. C., 1047.

" Mr. Beversham, the Master of the 'Lyon,' presented himself. The " Court askt him what became of the Portugal Commander, Ruy Frere, " and by what means he escaped, the Master made answere that it was " through the negligence of the watch; that he had sett a guard of six " men with rapiers and pistolls, and had given commandment that the " skiff should be moored astern, but, contrary to his direccon, it was left " by the shippe's side and he got awaie."—Court Minutes, 25th July 1628.

Everything was to be held as of secondary importance to its recovery. In 1639
D. R., Livro 46, fol. 1. orders were sent from Lisbon that the Dutch were to be, by all means, prevented from having intercourse with Persia or Sind; and attempts were to be made to get back Ormuz by treaty or otherwise.

Troubles now began to fall thick and fast upon the Portuguese in the Persian
D. R., Livro 47, fol. 20. Gulf. In 1640 certain Arabs, employed in the Custom House at Muscat, having informed the Imaum of the undefended condition of that fortress, owing to the majority of the soldiers having been sent away with the fleet, he attacked the place, but was repulsed by its garrison with considerable loss. On the
D. R., Livro 48, fol. 290. 7th November 1643 the Imaum took Soar, killing the guard and taking 37 prisoners. On the 16th
D. R., Livro 59, fol. 68. August 1648 the Arabs under Saide Ben Califa besieged Muscat, which held out until the 11th September, on which date a meeting of the Council decided that an attempt should be made to negotiate a treaty of peace, as the Portuguese had expended nearly all their ammunition. The conditions proposed by the enemy were that Curiate and the fortress of Dobar should be surrendered and razed to the ground; that the new fortress built by the Arabs at Matera should be recognized; that the merchants of the highlands should not pay duty at the Custom House at Muscat; that the wall of Muscat should be razed to the ground, and that the expenses of the war, amounting to 200,000 pardaos, should be paid by the Imaum. The Council declined to accede to these terms, and the siege accordingly continued until, disheartened by the fact that the hills of Mocala had been surrendered to the Arabs without a struggle, the plague being rife in

Muscat, with a mortality of 50 a day, and the ammunition being completely exhausted, the Captain General, on the 31st October, concluded negotiations with the Arab Captain and the siege was raised. The terms of capitulation agreed to were as follows :—

That the Portuguese should raze to the ground the fortresses of Curiate, Dobar, and Matera, and that the Imaum should similarly destroy the Arab fortress at the latter place; that Matera should belong to neither, and both parties were to be free to take away their artillery and baggage; that the Imaum's vessels should navigate outwards without reserve, and on the homeward voyage with passports from the King of Portugal; the vassals of the Imaum to pay no duties, either personal or upon merchandise, entering or leaving Muscat; commerce to be entirely and unrestrictedly free; the Arabs to take down any fortifications erected during the siege, and the Portuguese to bind themselves not to raise anything on the site of the demolished fortifications.

D. R., Livro 61, fol. 57.

Commenting upon these terms in a letter of the 16th March 1650, the King ordered inquiries to be made regarding the conduct of Dom Julião de Noronha, Captain General, and of the Vedor of the Finances of Muscat, for having made arrangements with the Arabs 15 days before the arrival of relief sent by the Viceroy. They were both accordingly made prisoners and sent to Goa.

D. R., Livro 60, fols. 48, 49.

In letters from the King of the 11th and 16th January 1649, reviewing the position of affairs in the Persian Gulf, His Majesty complained of a want of more vessels and sailors in Muscat, since no assistance could then be obtained from Soar and Caurusar as those places had been lost. Every effort was to be made to retain Muscat, and as Soar, Dobar, and Curiate were now no longer in the possession of the Portuguese, an endeavour should be made to open a port at Bandaly, in Persia, a short distance from Comorão. The fortress of Cassapo being in danger from the enemy should be strengthened. A great danger to Muscat, which His Majesty pointed out, was having Sheiks and Moors living inside the walls of the town, as they only acted as spies to inform the enemy of the condition of the Portuguese there.

On the 18th January 1650, the Viceroy received a letter from Diu informing him that a vessel had arrived there with 700 persons from Muscat, sent by the Captain General of that town, because the Arabs had entered it at night, killing a large number of people who had offered no resistance, no guard having been kept although for some time past it had been besieged by the Arabs. This turned out to be true; and it appears that, being hard pressed, the General retired to the fort commanding the town, leaving all the provisions, munitions, and arms in the factory, although his orders had been to keep depôts in both places. The Viceroy immediately ordered off a fleet to the relief, but when it arrived it was found that the fort had been surrendered on the 23rd and the factory on the 26th January to a very small force of Arabs. The Arabs in the Portuguese service fought, it is stated, with great bravery, but it was alleged that the surrender of Muskat must have been predetermined by the Captain General, the fleet also that was there having fled to Diu without making the least attempt to recover the place. It was at this time that vessels were sent to Persia to endeavour to obtain Ormuz, or some other situation on the Persian coast, and to procure the assistance of Persia against the Arabs. As a result of an inquiry instituted relative to the loss of Muscat, Braz Caldeira de Mattos, the Captain of the Fleet, had fled to Cochin, where he was in hiding in native territory. Having been found guilty he would have been

D. R., Livro 60, fol. 331.

D. R., Livro 60, fol. 339.

sentenced to capital punishment, but being a Cavalheiro of a military order he was beyond the jurisdiction of the Viceroy.

After the fall of Muscat, the Viceroy sent seven galliots to the Straits of Ormuz. These went first to Sind and Kongo, at which latter place they took in provisions and then proceeded to El Katiff. The fleet then appears to have visited the Khan of Lara, with the view of obtaining from him a cession of Ormuz or of Larack. As soon as they had left Kongo the Arabs arrived there with a large fleet and captured three patachos off that place, having first fought and captured a vessel which had got separated from the fleet. Shortly afterwards the Arabs captured more merchant vessels; and, in consequence of these losses the reputation of the Portuguese fell considerably in the estimation of the neighbouring kings. It was accordingly felt to be of the first importance to send a strong fleet to destroy the Arab vessels in the Persian Gulf. Persia had offered a site to the Portuguese for a fortification on the island of Angao if a fleet of six vessels were sent to occupy it; but the Viceroy hoped that if a larger fleet were sent he would give a more advantageous site, such as Cassapo.

D. R., Livro 61, fol. 578.

A strong Portuguese fleet entered the Straits of Ormuz on the 16th March 1652, and off Muscat encountered an Arab armada which placed itself under the guns of that fortress. It was alleged that the Portuguese might then have easily destroyed the Arab vessels and have probably even recaptured Muscat, but the captain seems to have shirked an encounter, and to have thus lost the opportunity of re-establishing the Portuguese power in the Persian Gulf, which never again appears to have presented itself to the representatives of that race which had, for so many years, been the paramount ruler in those seas.

D. R., Livro 56, fol. 466.

The eighteenth century opened with new hopes for the Portuguese of recovering their position in the Persian Gulf. The Shah of Persia having recently lost Ormuz, which had been taken by the Turks, and Bahrein by the Arabs, sent an Ambassador to Goa to request the assistance of the Portuguese against those enemies. Accordingly a fleet was sent to Bander Kongo, in February 1719; and on the 4th August an Arab fleet appeared off that port. On the morning of the next day both fleets weighed anchor and put out to sea. The fight commenced at 9 a.m., and continued until 7 p.m., when the enemy retired in good order, and advantage was taken of the night by both sides to repair damages. The engagement recommenced at 6 a.m. the next morning, the enemy proceeding through the Straits followed by the Portuguese fleet, and a running fight was kept up for the entire day until night again separated the combatants. At daybreak the next morning the enemy was discovered at some distance, but on the Portuguese fleet giving chase, retired precipitately, declining to renew the battle, and took refuge amongst the islands and shoals of the Straits, where the Portuguese, unaccustomed to the navigation, were unable to follow. The next day (the 8th August) the enemy being no longer in sight, the Portuguese Admiral returned to his original anchorage in the Port of Kongo. The loss of the enemy is supposed to have been 500 killed and wounded, whilst the Portuguese had only 10 killed and 35 wounded. News shortly afterwards reached the Portuguese Admiral that the Arabs had put into the Port of Jalfar, 20 leagues off, to repair and await reinforcements, both from Muscat, and from the English and Dutch, who were said to be at Bander Bassein, and he accordingly resolved to seek them out at their anchorage, for which purpose he

Evora Cod. CIII., 3–16, fol. 58 vo.

Evora Cod. CXV., 1–38, fol. 309.

started with four ships on the 27th August. On the 29th he came in sight of the enemy, who at once retired, being chased by the Portuguese, but night coming on the fight only lasted one hour. On the 30th the day broke with a calm and the enemy in sight, but it was not until mid-day that the wind freshened sufficiently for the vessels to approach one another. At 1 p.m. the battle commenced, and by nightfall the enemy had been completely routed. On the 31st the two fleets again came within sight of one another, but the Arabs took to flight, chased by the Portuguese who, from want of wind, were unable to overtake them. All through the next day the chase continued, and on the 2nd September the Arabs finally retired from the Straits and took refuge in their own ports. On the 5th the Portuguese fleet returned to Kongo.

This signal defeat of the Arabs was followed by riots in Muscat; and the death of the Imaum, who was succeeded by his nephew, was followed by an attempt on the part of the latter to negotiate a peace with the Portuguese, which, however, they declined to agree to. Finding that the King of Persia, who had been successful in his domestic wars in consequence of this maritime diversion, gave no sign of besieging Muscat, as he had promised to do, the Portuguese fleet wintered in the Persian ports, and withdrew to Goa at the end of the year.

PORTUGUESE INDIA.

Section VI.

CEYLON.

Dom Francisco de Almeida, the first Viceroy of India, left Lisbon with a fleet on the 25th March 1505, arriving at Angediva on the 12th September, at Cananor on the 24th October, and at Cochin on the 1st November following, where he established his principal residence, and thus constituted it the seat of Portuguese Government in India.* By this time the Portuguese vessels had driven away the Moorish ships from the Malabar coast, and those from the Persian Gulf or Red Sea, desiring to proceed to Malacca or Sumatra, finding they could no longer with safety follow their former course down the Indian coast, adopted a fresh route keeping outside the Laccadive Islands, and passing through the Maldive group so as to avoid the Portuguese cruisers. This fact having come to the knowledge of the Viceroy, he fitted out a fleet of nine ships which he placed under the command of his son, Dom Lourenço, with instructions to stop this route also to the Moorish ships. Dom Lourenço sailed from Cochin for the Maldives at the end of 1505 or early in 1506,† but as the pilots were quite

* Ensaios sobre a Estatistica das possessoẽs Portuguezas no ultramar.

† Almost without exception English historians state that Ceylon was discovered by the Portuguese in 1505, and some Portuguese authorities have adopted the same date. No exact date is, however, anywhere given of the sailing of Dom Lourenço's fleet, and the only attempt at an approximate time is stated by Antonio Galvano, who says it was "no fim deste anno [1505], ou na entrada do outro." According to the *Rajawali* the Portuguese first arrived at Ceylon in the month of April, and the error in that case cannot have been due to the practice then existing of making the year end on the 24th March.

ignorant* of the navigation of those parts, after cruising about for 18 days without seeing the islands, they were driven by the currents towards Ceylon, where by chance they fetched the chief port of the island, called Colombo,† which Dom Lourenço entered. Here he found ships from various parts loading with cinnamon and elephants; he was well received by the King, with whom he concluded a treaty of friendship and trade, under which the former agreed to pay tribute in cinnamon and elephants to the King of Portugal who, in return, was to protect Ceylon from all enemies.

I have been unable to find any copy or even extracts of this treaty, and some doubt has been thrown upon the responsibility of the person with whom it was concluded. It appears, however, pretty certain that after Dom Lourenço's visit no other Portuguese vessel went to Ceylon until it was visited by the Governor Lopo Soares de Albergaria. He arrived at Galle on the 27th September 1518,‡ and proceeded thence to Colombo, where he was well received by the Emperor of whom he demanded the tribute which he had granted to Dom Lourenço, and also obtained from him a site for the erection of a wooden palisade for the better protection of a warehouse. Here he left a garrison of 200 men with four pinnaces, and then returned to India. Two years later he despatched thence some vessels with men and materials for the erection of a stone fort in the place of the wooden palisade. This was completed without much opposition, but the Emperor appears subsequently to have entertained apprehensions as to the real object of its erection and he closely besieged the place

---

* Lendas da India, T. I., Part II., p. 646.

† Noticias ultramarinas; Lendas da India, T. II., Pt. II., p. 539; Castanheda, Vol. IV., p. 94; Ensaios, p. 15.

‡ Castanheda says (Vol. II., p. 73) Dom Lourenço cruised round the island and entered the port of Gabaliquama, now called Galle, where he was well received by the King, who agreed to pay an annual tribute to the King of Portugal.

for some time, but on the arrival of reinforcements from India he was forced to retire, and he shortly afterwards agreed to terms of peace.

The Portuguese had now obtained a firm foothold in Ceylon, whence they continually carried on petty wars with the King of Kandy.

The King of Cotta was nominally the paramount sovereign of Ceylon. Bhuwaneka VII., who succeeded to the throne in 1534, being very much pressed, owing to the rebellion of certain of his subjects led by his brother Maaya Dunnai (called by the Portuguese Madune), sought the assistance of the Portuguese, and obtained from them a guarantee of succession to the sovereignty for his grandson Dharmapala* Bahu, in return for which a party of Franciscan priests from Portugal were permitted to preach Christianity throughout the island. These arrived in 1542, and succeeded in establishing communities of converts in various parts along the coast, including Paneture, Calituré, Maça, Barberin, Galle, and Belligaum, where the Portuguese already possessed trading stations.† In the last-mentioned year Bhuwaneka VII. was accidentally killed, and was succeeded by his grandson, who appears to have retained his possessions for twelve years, but in 1564 the warlike son of Maaya Dunnai, Raja Singha, attacked Cotta with such energy that on the advice of the Portuguese the fortress was dismantled, and the King retired to Colombo where he continued to reside for the remainder of his days. Here he embraced the Christian religion, adopting the name of Dom João, and before his death he executed a deed making

---

* Dharmapala, when raised to the throne, was baptized, and adopted the name of Dom João. A statue of him had previously been sent to Lisbon, which was crowned by King Dom João III. with a golden crown.

† Faria-y-Sousa, Vol. 2, pt. 2, ch. XII.

over his territories to the Kings of Portugal.* On his death, in 1597, the inhabitants of Ceylon swore allegiance to D. Phillipe, then King of Portugal.

D. R., Livro 51, fol. 370.

The Portuguese had a fort at Manar, which is stated

---

* Bequest which the King of Ceylon makes of his Territories to the Kings of Portugal. (Livro das Ilhas, fol. 238. Collecção de Tratados, &c., Vol. I., p. 180):—

"Made this 12th day of August 1580, in the city and fortress of Colombo, in the dwelling of His Highness Prince Dom Joam, by the grace of God King of Ceylon. Perea Pandar (Emperor), the aforesaid King, being present, states to me, Antonio Ribeiro, Notary Public of His Majesty the King (of Portugal), Lord of this city, in the presence of witnesses, that he, the King, succeeded to these kingdoms of Ceylon on the death of King Bonegabao (Bhuwaneka VII.), his lord and grandfather, who had no children, and had during his lifetime adopted him as his son, and made him heir with the sanction of the King of Portugal, Dom Joam III.; and further states that he possessed these kingdoms in the same way as the aforesaid Bonegabao, his grandfather, having his seat in the royal city of Cotta, the capital of the kingdom now dismantled; and that afterwards, through various causes, the Madume Pandar (Maaya Dunnai), King of Suita Avaca (Ceitavaca), and the Rajuu (Raja Singha), his son, had tyrannically occupied and taken possession of all his kingdoms, leaving him only with the city and fortress of Colombo, which the Kings of Portugal, through their Viceroys and captains, defended for a long time in order to restore the said Kingdoms to him, which restoration they had however been unable to carry out in consequence of other wars the Viceroys were engaged in and the impoverished state of India, and . . . He, the King, is advanced in years and in failing health, without sons and heirs to rightfully succeed him at his death, and feeling greatly indebted to the Kings of Portugal for all their mercies and help, and especially for the comforts of religion ministered to him by their priests, whereby he was converted to the Catholic faith. . . . He, the King, bequeaths to the King of Portugal, Dom Manuel, and his heirs, all his kingdoms and lands with the hope that he will obtain possession of those kingdoms which are now in the hands of his enemies, giving him permission to fight his enemies by sea and land until he obtain possession of all the territories which he had a right to in the same manner as the Kings of Cotta had reigned over the other Kings in this island, &c."

This document was signed by the King, the witnesses being Friar Sebastião de Chaves, Manuel Luiz, priest, Estevam Figueira, Pero Jorge Frauquo, Antonio Lawrenço, and Captain Manuel de Souza Coutinho.

by Rezende to have been founded by Soares de Albergaria in 1518. A fortress was also erected at Batecalou by Constantino de Saa de Noronha in 1528, and one at Galle by order of the Viceroy, Mathias de Albuquerque, in 1589. These, however, appear to have been of but little account until a later date, since Van Linschoten, who was in India from 1583 until 1592, remarked that in "Seylon " . . . lyeth a fort belonging to the Portugals, " called Columbo, which by meere force and great " charges is holden (and maintained), for that they " have no other (place or peece of ground) no not one " foot, but that in all the Iland."*

MSS. in Bibliotheca Nacional, Lisbon, Vol. A 2, 29.

In 1587 the fort of Colombo was besieged by the Raja Singha (King of Ceitavaca), who tried to become possessed of the King of Cotta's† dominions. The garrison was reduced to great straits, and on the 4th October the Raja's fleet arrived off the port, where it was immediately engaged by all the Portuguese vessels available, and defeated with great loss. Reinforcements in the meanwhile arrived from Goa in time to resist the final attack, which was made by the Raja's forces on the 10th January 1588, and continued until the 15th without success. On the 17th, another onslaught was made on the fort, when the Raja's forces were totally defeated and forced to retire.

From the beginning of the seventeenth century the Portuguese assumed authority over the greater part of the island, with the exception of Kandy and Uva, which they had already recognized as independent kingdoms belonging to the Queen Catherina and her heirs. After many years of bloodshed and war, having somewhat

* "The Voyage of John Huyghen Van Linschoten to the East Indies," Vol. 1, p. 76.—*Hakluyt Society's publications.*

† De Couto, T. 10, pt. 2, p. 580.

consolidated their power, the Portuguese began to give a little settled government to the country.

"Foral de Ceylão" and "Foral de Jafanapatão."

Upon assuming the sovereignty of the land the Imperial taxes all went into the Royal Treasury. The land tax was usually calculated at the rate of 12 per cent. of the gross produce, of which one-third was required to be paid in pepper, and two thirds in money. Besides this assessment, the tenant of each holding appraised at 50 pardaos* was bound to have one gun or musket, to be available for the service of the State, and those possessing holdings assessed at from 50 to 100 pardaos were to have one gun and one bow, with a proper supply of arrows. From 100 pardaos upwards, one gun and one bow extra were required to be provided for every additional 100 pardaos. All lands valued at less than 50 pardaos had to provide one lance. Whenever the soil was favourable to their growth, pepper trees had to be cultivated under pain of loss of tenancy. The working of quarries in the district of Dinavaca was limited to four months, from the 1st January to the end of April in each year, and then it was only permitted to be carried on in the presence of a "viduna" (or overseer) and an assistant, who had to enter in a register the precious stones (catseyes and sapphires) as they were discovered. The stones were then taxed according to their weight and estimated value. Potters had to pay a tax called "bada," and were compelled to make tiles for State works. Revenue was also obtained from the "marallas," a very ancient royal tax, claimed by Kings on the death of any one. It consisted of one-third part of the personal property of the deceased.

Elephant hunting was considered the most important thing, after cinnamon, in Ceylon, and both were claimed as royal properties, and forbidden without a license.

---

* The pardao is supposed to have been worth about 4*s*. 2*d*. to 4*s*. 6*d*.

The right of elephant hunting in one part of the island, consisting of 44 villages, which had from time immemorial been held under native Kings by a certain caste of elephant hunters, was continued to them in consideration of an annual tribute of 30 elephants' heads with tusks, otherwise called "royal elephants."

All imports and exports at the several ports had to pay a customs duty at the rate of 7 per cent. *ad valorem*.

In 1609 André Furtado de Mendonça, the Viceroy, took* possession of the entire Kingdom of Jafanapatam, and on the death of D. Catharina, Portuguese troops were sent to take possession of the kingdom of Kandy; they were however repulsed, but on the 24th August 1617 a treaty was signed with the King of Kandy, under which, in return for an acknowledgment of his sovereignty by the King of Portugal, he agreed to pay a tribute of two elephants yearly, to suppress any rising within his dominions, to give up all the Portuguese taken at Balané, to send as hostages people of position, and to release all captives who might be Christians. In 1618 a fort was erected at Jafanapatam.

Tratados, T. I., p. 203.

Rezende MSS.

On the arrival of Constantino de Saa de Noronha as Captain General of Ceylon in 1623,† the first thing he did was to build a fort at Trinquimalé, and, in 1628, he erected another at the port of Batecalou. This gave great offence to the King of Kandy, who accordingly declared war against the Portuguese, but was defeated, whereupon he retired on Uva, and the enemy entering Kandy burnt the city. In the following year (1629), the King of Kandy moved his army against Jafanapatam, but on the arrival there of reinforcements that place was relieved. He then sued

* "Ensaios," p. 116.

† "Noticias Ultramarinas," T. V., p. 76.

for peace, which the Portuguese Governor agreed to, but the King's army almost immediately treacherously fell upon the Portuguese troops, and nearly annihilated them, and the Governor Constantino de Saa de Noronha was amongst the slain. Reinforcements were speedily sent to Colombo and Galle from Cochin, Malacca, and Goa, which reached there in October 1631. The Portuguese authority was thus re-established, and on the 15th April 1633 a treaty of peace was concluded with Maastana the King, and signed at Goa, on the following terms:—

Tratados, T. II., p. 38.

That the dominions of Kandy shall be divided among three kings, sons of Queen D. Catharina, lawful heiress of these territories, and as Kandy is the principal kingdom, he, the King Maastana, is the chief; that all thieves be handed over to either side, together with their plunder; that neither side break the peace and declare war without giving notice, and the reasons for doing so; that the fortress of Batecalou be the property of Portugal, but the land about it the property of the King, who is, however, not to approach within 2,000 paces of the fort; that the King of Kandy's tribute of two elephants be reduced to one elephant per annum for six years; that a prelate of the Order of S. Francisco be allowed to reside in Kandy, to minister to the religious wants of any Christians who may be there; and that on peace being signed the King of Kandy shall give up all captains and other Portuguese whom he may have as prisoners.

In the year 1637 the Danes endeavoured to establish a factory in Ceylon, but this was vigorously opposed by the Portuguese Viceroy, and they were in consequence unsuccessful. Later on in the year, the President of the Danish Company informed the Viceroy that the Dutch were preparing forces to blockade Malacca, Ceylon, and

D. R., Livro 40, fol. 231, 375.
Livro 41, fol. 11.
„ 43 „ 195.

Goa, and he offered to assist the Portuguese in the defence of Tranquebar or Negapatam, in consideration of his Company being allowed to settle a factory in Ceylon. This offer, however, appears to have led to no better results, for it appears that in the following year the Danes renewed their offer to assist the Portuguese against the Dutch in Ceylon if they would permit them to buy areca, elephants, and cinnamon there; but the Portuguese council considered that this offer could not be entertained without a treaty being first entered into for that purpose by their respective kings. Notwithstanding these repeated refusals, in April 1638 the President of the Danish Company sent provisions and ammunition to the Portuguese in Ceylon, which, for some unexplained reason, seem never to have reached them; he further offered to send money to pay their soldiers if the Portuguese would agree to let him purchase elephants and cinnamon at a fair price, but I have been unable to find any evidence that this request was more favourably received than those previously made.

Although they had no claim to the kingdom, the Portuguese evidently maintained a camp in Kandy, or its neighbourhood, for it is stated in "Noticias Ultramarinas"* that on the death of the Maastaná he was succeeded by his son Raja Singha as King of Kandy, who shortly afterwards fell out with the Portuguese, and in an engagement that followed the latter were defeated and lost their encampment there. After this the King sent representatives to Batavia with a view to entering into an alliance with the Dutch, in consequence of which a Dutch fleet left Goa for Ceylon in February 1639, and six other vessels proceeded about the same time from Batavia with orders to attack the Portuguese forts at Batecalou† and Trin-

D. R., Livro 44, fol. 252.

* "Noticias Ultramarinas," T. V., p. 88.

† "Noticias Ultramarinas," T. V., p. 93.

quimalé, which they destroyed with the greatest ease.

D. R., Livro 41, fol. 9, vo.
„ Livro 47, fol. 74.
„ Livro 48, fol. 70, vo.
„ Livro 46, fol. 151.

The former was taken on the 15th August 1639, and the latter in the following year. The capture of these forts placed the whole island almost within the grasp of the Dutch, and orders were accordingly sent out from Lisbon that every effort should be made to deprive them of their positions there. To further harass them, the Mataran (one of the Kings of Java) was to be induced not to make peace with them, and to this end the Viceroy was instructed to hold out prospects of assistance to him, without however compromising himself too far in the matter.

In the middle of January 1640 a fleet of 12 Dutch vessels appeared off Colombo;* troops were landed near a village called Caimel, north of Negumbo, and the fort at the latter place was captured without any resistance, it being garrisoned only by aged men. Galle was next attacked, and here the Portuguese were totally defeated and the fortress was also captured.

On the arrival of the Conde de Aveiras João da Silva Tello as Viceroy, he appointed D. Antonio Mascarenhas as Captain General of Ceylon. He arrived with a fleet near Negumbo on the night of the 24th October 1640 and, having landed troops, besieged the place, which surrendered on the 4th November, and a treaty of capitulation was signed on the 9th idem.

D. R., Livro 47, fols. 86, 87.

Upon the accession of King João IV. to the throne of Portugal, in December 1640, a treaty of alliance was concluded with the States General, in which it was stipulated, with regard to India and the East, as follows:—

This document provided for an inviolable treaty of peace between the King and the States General, on the

Tratados, T. II., p. 108.

* "Noticias Ultramarinas, T. V., p. 95.

seas as well as on land, for a period of ten years from the 12th June 1641, the date on which it was signed. In India, however, it was not to come into force until one year later; but should the proclamation of peace arrive there earlier, all acts of hostilities between the two nations were to cease at once. All the kings, sovereigns, and nations in the East Indies who might be friends of, or in confederation with, the States General, or the Dutch East India Company, were to be included in this treaty. The subjects of that Company were to enjoy, in the dominions of the King of Portugal, the same exemptions and liberties and rights as the other subjects of that State enjoyed under this treaty, provided the East India Company and its subjects did not convey from Brazil, sugar, Brazilian wood, or any other Brazilian product to the kingdom of Portugal, and the Portuguese did not convey the same from Brazil to the said provinces. The Dutch and Portuguese were to aid each other, should occasion arise, during the continuance of this treaty. The subjects and inhabitants of the territories of Dom João IV., and those of the States General respectively, were, during the ten years peace herein provided for, to profess friendship and forget all injuries and wrongs they might have suffered.

D. R., Livro 48, fol. 53.

In anticipation of the signing of the aforesaid treaty, the King of Portugal wrote to the Viceroy, on the 18th March 1641, directing him to inform the authorities in India that the causes of war between the Portuguese and Dutch had now ceased, that an armistice was to be declared, and that no hostilities were to be commenced pending further orders. The Native Princes were also to be informed that there would now be no further wars between the Europeans in India. The Dutch, however, do not appear to have acted in the

D. R., Livro 48, fol. 117.

same loyal manner, for, under the excuse that no official notification had reached Batavia of the ratification of the treaty between Portugal and Holland, they were, in the beginning of February 1643, preparing an expedition to fall upon Colombo with the aid of the King of Kandy. On the 2nd March following, the Dutch Commissioner, Pedro Boreel, arrived in India with the armistice, and proceeded first to Galle, where, however, he declined to publish it on the ground that, as the Dutch were entirely hemmed* in there at that time, he thought it best that the fight should continue. He then proceeded to Goa, where he arrived on the 1st April, and here also he declined to publish the armistice, unless the Portuguese would first give up the lands around Galle, giving the following reasons for not including Galle in the armistice:—

D. R., Livro 48, fol. 151.

"1. When I arrived at Ceylon the Portuguese forces were in our lands subject to the kingdom of Galle, in which they possessed no fortress whatever, and to which, therefore, they could have no right; being called upon by me, they declined to evacuate the same lands.

D. R., Livro 51, fol. 322.

"2. Being also called upon by me to leave us in free possession of the lands of Saffragão, which, as well as those of Galle, are mortgaged to us by the Emperor of Ceylon, Raja Singha, for a large sum of money spent on His Majesty's behalf, they also refused, and that, in spite of their not possessing any fortress whatever there, the lands being now under the Government of the Emperor of the Island of Ceylon, Raja Singha."

The Viceroy in reply denied that these lands belonged to the Emperor at all; he could not therefore mortgage them, and he

D. R., Livro 51, fol. 324.
" " 48, fol. 151.

* It would appear that, on obtaining possession of Baticalou and Trinquimalé, the Dutch destroyed the fortresses at those places, for, writing on the 4th December 1643, the Viceroy stated that the only fortress possessed by the Dutch in Ceylon was that of Galle, and that they were so hemmed in there that they could not put their feet outside of it; he also stated that the Portuguese were in absolute possession of the rest of the island.

D. R., Livro 48, fol. 127.

accordingly refused to surrender them. Pedro Boreel thereupon returned on board his vessel on the 23rd April, declaring that the war would remain on the same footing as before. Against this the Viceroy entered a solemn protest, and suggested, as a possible solution of the difficulty, that the King of Portugal should purchase the fortress of Galle, which might, he thought, with advantage be paid for in cinnamon. Pending negotiations to this end, however, he requested that a peremptory order might be obtained from the States General ordering the armistice to be observed in India. After leaving Goa without proclaiming the armistice, Pedro Boreel proceeded to Galle, where he arrived on the 8th May 1643, and disembarked 300 men, who, being joined by a part of the garrison, established a camp outside the walls of the fortress. Next morning he sent a messenger to the Portuguse Captain General renewing the declaration of war, and on the 10th he marched against the Portuguese camp, but met with a most decisive defeat and was obliged to retire. He embarked the remainder of his forces in a vessel he had left in Belligaum Bay, and proceeded to Tanjore, in the hope of being able to induce the Naique to assist him against the Portuguese. On the Naique's refusal to join the Dutch in this enterprise, Pedro Boreel went to Paliacate, and a few days after his arrival there was found dead in his bed.

D. R., Livro 48, fol. 266.

The Portuguese forces continued the siege of Galle, but, on the news of the defeat of the Dutch reaching Batavia, a reinforcement was sent thence for the relief of that fort.

On the 27th September 1643 five Dutch vessels arrived at Goa, and the captain of the fleet informed the Viceroy that he was authorized to arrange the armistice, on condition that half the lands previously claimed between Galle and Colombo were surrendered. Ne-

D. R., Livro 48, fol. 268.

gotiations followed, but, as the Viceroy refused to entertain any proposal for the surrender of lands in Ceylon, the Dutch captain suggested, as an alternative, an armistice for one year from Cape Comorin to the point of Diu. As this would have excluded Ceylòn, the coast of Coromandel, and China, this proposal was also declined.

D. R., Livro 48, fol. 290.

A Dutch fleet of fourteen vessels arrived off Galle on the 22nd December 1643 and sailed up the coast, whereupon the Captain of the forces besieging Galle raised his camp and retired upon Colombo, whence he was ordered to take up a position upon a small island in front of Negumbo. Shortly afterwards the enemy's fleet hove in sight, and disembarked some troops within gunshot of that fortress, whereupon two officers commanding the Portuguese forces, disobeying superior orders, rushed to attack them in a disorderly manner, and in less than two hours were defeated with a loss of 300 men, amongst whom were both these captains. The fortress was thus retaken by the Dutch on the 3rd January 1644, and the Captain General, with the remains of his force, returned to Colombo.

D. R., Livro 56, fol. 258.

Tratados, T. II., p. 175.

The treaty between the Dutch and Portuguese of June 1641 was at last published in Goa on the 10th November 1644. A provisional treaty was shortly afterwards agreed to, between the King of Portugal and the States General, respecting certain doubts as to the jurisdiction of the territories of the fortress of Galle, which was signed at the Hague on the 27th March 1645. The possessors of that fort were to have the use of the lands in the same way as they had at the time the Treaty of 1641 was signed, but they were not to grow cinnamon while the dispute lasted, during which time, however, the King of Portugal agreed to deliver annually to the said fort 600 quintals (about 30 tons) of that spice. The King of Portugal and the States General were to consider the dispute and settle the matter, but, in the event of their failing to agree, the question was to be submitted to arbitration, and all vessels and goods seized, as well as places and forts taken by either party since the Treaty of 1641 was proclaimed, were to be immediately restored. In accordance with this treaty an arrangement was made for the division of the lands of Ceylon between the two States, under which Colombo was to have seven provinces attached to it, Negumbo eight, and certain other provinces were to be divided between them. The division between Colombo and Galle was to be the River Alecan, which river and its fort were to remain in the possession of the Portuguese, with a right reserved to the Dutch of using the river. The Portuguese Viceroy, whilst agreeing to this division with the view of preventing farther bloodshed, protested against it as not being in accordance with the letter of the Treaty.

After this, war seems to have been carried on incessantly by the Dutch and King of Kandy against the Portuguese, and repeated engagements ensued without however leading to any practical attainment until March 1654, when, as the result of a rather severe encounter, a Dutch* army was badly defeated, and the Portuguese took Caliture, which they at once occupied. In September 1655 a powerful Dutch fleet arrived off that place and bombarded it, and after a siege of eleven days the commander agreed to a capitulation, owing to the garrison being without provisions. The terms of the capitulation were, that the soldiers and non-commissioned officers should be sent to Batavia, and from thence be transhipped to Holland; the Captains were to be sent to Persia, and the Captain-Mor, Antonio Mendes Aranha, to Galle. With these conditions the fortress was surrendered on the 14th October 1655.

* "Noticias Ultramarinas," T. V., fol. 164.

In the last-mentioned year proposals passed between the English and Portuguese for a union of interests, with the view of driving the Dutch out of India. Circumstances at the time, however, prevented the realization of this project, but the Portuguese, having prepared a fleet, despatched it to Ceylon, and it arrived at Colombo on the 23rd March. Off the bar of that port they met three large Dutch ships, to which they gave fight; two of these were run ashore, but the third succeeded in getting into Negumbo. After this the Portuguese fleet proceeded to blockade Galle, which place they also besieged by land. The land force on its way met with a body of Dutch troops from Caliture, who, after a brisk engagement, retired upon Galle, destroying the roads and bridges as they went. The Portuguese, however, refrained from following up the advantage they had here obtained over their enemies.

Evora Cod. C.V., 2—15, fol. 46.

After a series of engagements with Dutch troops in the neighbourhood of Colombo, the Portuguese retired into that fortress and prepared for a siege. The enemy began to attack the fort on the 28th October 1655, and, after a bombardment by land and sea for fifteen days, they succeeded in getting a ship into the bay during the night of the 12th November. When, however, the Dutch troops began their final attack, the vessel ran aground and was captured, and every assault on the walls during the next two days was repulsed with great slaughter. The siege* was continued with great perseverance, and at last, early in May 1656, it was decided at a Council to capitulate, and at 3 p.m. on the 12th of that month the remains of the Portuguese garrison, consisting only of 73 men, proceeded to the headquarters of the Dutch General and gave themselves up. After the loss of

Evora Cod. CV., 2—15, fol. 46.

---

* "Noticias Ultramarinas," T. V., p. 200.

Colombo, the Portuguese sent reinforcements to the island of Manar and the kingdom of Jafanapatam. Accordingly, in the middle of February 1658, the Dutch sent a force of ten ships and 3,200 men to dislodge them from thence. They landed a force on Manar without opposition, and then proceeded to Jafanapatam, which place was resolutely defended from the 20th March to the 22nd June, but, running short of provisions and ammunition, the garrison was at last forced to surrender, and Jafanapatam was given up to the Dutch General on the 24th June 1658. Thus ended the territorial possessions of Portugal in Ceylon, just 152 years after their first arrival in that island.

PORTUGUESE INDIA.

SECTION VII.

MALACCA.

During* the Vice-royalty of D. Francisco d'Almeida, in May 1509, four ships arrived at Goa from Lisbon, under the command of Diogo Lopes de Sequeira, with instructions to discover the island of San Laurenço,† and if he found the cloves and drugs spoken of by Tristão da Cunha he was to load and return to Portugal, but, if not, he was to proceed to the discovery of Malacca and demand tribute. Diogo Lopes went to San Laurenço, but finding nothing there he began his voyage to Malacca, and on the way put in to Cochin owing to stress of weather. The vessels, after repairing and taking in Cochin pilots, resumed their voyage in August 1509. Diogo Lopes also took with him some slaves who spoke the Malacca tongue, and being favoured with fine weather reached his destination in safety. On the arrival of this expedition the King sent off to inquire the object of the visit, to which Diogo Lopes replied that he had come for trading purposes, and also in the hope that the King would conclude a treaty with Portugal, after the manner of the Kings of Cochin, Cananor, Ceylon, and Melinde.

The King was pleased with this response, and gave the Portuguese permission to land and trade with his people, whereupon Diogo Lopes sent on shore a merchant, named Ruy de Aranjo, with presents for the

* "Lendas da India," T. I., p. 971 ; T. II., p. 32.
† Madagascar.

King, and instructions to obtain from His Majesty some houses as near the water as possible. This request was complied with, and Ruy de Araujo, accompanied by eight companions, settled themselves there, and carried on a very large trade with the Natives. This naturally raised the jealousy of the Moorish merchants, who took every opportunity of exciting the King's suspicions against the Portuguese, telling him that they always adopted the method of introducing themselves to foreign nations as peaceful merchants, and after a time declared war and made the people vassals. These representations had the desired effect, and the King accordingly made preparations to massacre the Portuguese, for which purpose, about two months after their first arrival at Malacca, he equipped a large fleet behind a woody island not far from that town. A night was fixed on for an attack on the factory, but the Portuguese had been put on their guard by a Native woman who was on terms of friendship with one of the men in the place. Having thus warned the factory, she swam to the boats moored off the town, by whom the alarm was conveyed to the Portuguese ships. The attack speedily followed, and those in the factory made a stubborn resistance, but were overpowered and forced to surrender. The Portuguese ships bombarded the town during the night, but perceiving, on the morning, that the factory had been demolished, Diogo Lopes sent a boat ashore with a flag of truce. The boat was, however, fired on, and returned to the ships, whereupon the fleet set sail and returned to Colombo, whence Diogo Lopes, in one of his ships, returned to Lisbon and communicated to the King a most glowing account of the riches of Malacca.*

---

* Ludovico di Barthemy, who visited Malacca about this date, remarked :—" The city of Melacha is on the mainland, and pays tribute " to the King of Cini (Siam), who caused this place to be built about " 80 years ago, because there is a good port there, which is the prin- " cipal port of the main ocean. And truly I believe that more ships

An expedition, under Diogo Mendez de Vasconcellos, sailed from Lisbon, on the 12th March 1510, for the express purpose of conquering Malacca,* but, on his arrival at Goa, Affonso de Albuquerque, the Viceroy, determined to undertake the expedition himself. Accordingly he arrived there with a fleet in June 1511, and after some negotiation the King delivered up Ruy de Araujo and such of his companions as had not already escaped; but as he was making preparation for war, Albuquerque landed a large force on the 25th July 1511 and captured the place, where he at once erected a fort, and, leaving it in charge of Ruy de Brito with 300 men, he returned to India.

The letter from Affonso de Albuquerque, giving an account of this enterprise, is evidently not now in existence, as it is not contained in the volume of letters from him recently printed by the Portuguese Government. In a letter of the 1st April 1512 to the King he remarked,—

Cartas, T. I., p. 53.

"Malacca is a grand place, and is in such a situation that, even if no Malacca existed, it would be the duty of your Majesty to have a fortress, such is the trade there. Place ships and men there for one, two, three, and four years in order that your Majesty's name may be feared in those parts, and then they will desire your Majesty's friendship and agree to a treaty. I say this in order that the end may be accomplished without having recourse to war."

One of the earliest acts here of Affonso de Albuquerque appears to have been the issue of a Portuguese coinage, for in the same letter he states, "Nuno Vaz takes with him "samples of the gold, silver, and copper coins which have "been struck in your Majesty's name at Malacca." In

Cartas, T. I., p. 58.

"arrive here than in any other place in the world, and especially there "come here all sorts of spices and an immense quantity of other "merchandise."—*Hakluyt Society*, Vol. 32, p. 223.

* "Commentaries of Affonso de Albuquerque," Vol. II., p. 196; "Lendas da India," T. II., p. 219, *et seq.*

a subsequent letter of the 30th October 1512, Affonso de Albuquerque reminds the King that Malacca is one of his greatest treasures in the East, and begs his Majesty to send him ships, men, and arms, as well as artizans, and all the materials necessary for the construction of a good fortress.

Cartas, T. I., p. 97.

The Moors made desperate attempts to evict the Portuguese, in which they obtained assistance from Java, but the latter succeeded in maintaining their position. They were next attacked by the King of Bintang in 1518, but, with the aid of reinforcements, he also was driven from Pago,* where he had fortified himself, and he retired to his own island accompanied by the King of Malacca. Here he was unsuccessfully attacked by the Portuguese in 1521. War continued between the Portuguese and Bintang for some years, but in 1526 an expedition went from Malacca and entirely defeated the King of Bintang's forces, after which many neighbouring kings made treaties with the Portuguese, and Malacca prospered for some time.

In 1538 the King of Achin made an attack on Malacca, but was defeated with great loss. After this very little appears on the records relative to Malacca until the year 1572, when the Kings of the Deccan having formed a league against the Christians with the Zamorin and the King of Achin, the latter prepared a large fleet to attack Malacca, whereupon Luiz de Mello da Silva, with a fleet, met that of Achin, which he fought and conquered, and thus relieved Malacca from a siege. The Achinese, however, returned home, and at once made preparations for another attack, in which they invited the Queen of Japara to join them. The fol-

Evora. Cod., CXVI., 1—26.

* Pago was a fortress of the King of Bintang, a league up the River Muar, which is but a little south of Malacca.

lowing year (1573) the Achinese appeared before Malacca with a large fleet and 7,000 warriors, on the 13th October, and the same night disembarked part of their troops. A fearful storm arose and wrecked several of their vessels. Two days later they fought the Portuguese vessels in the port without any particular advantage, after which part of the fleet went to blockade the mouth of the River Muar, five leagues from the city, thus preventing the arrival of provisions by sea, upon which the fort was dependent. A new Governor arrived at Malacca on the 2nd November with a small escort, whereupon it was decided to attack the Achinese fleet. Battle was given on the 15th November off the mouth of the River Formosa,* when the Achinese fleet was routed with great loss. The Portuguese Admiral remained for three days on the spot, and then returned to Malacca.

On the 5th October 1574 Malacca was again besieged by a fleet of 300 vessels sent by the Queen of Japara. Part of the troops disembarked and drove the Portuguese into the fortress, killing many of them, after which the Japarese fleet was run into the river of the Malays (the Malabar river), whereupon the Portuguese sallied out and burnt 60 of them. The enemy now stockaded the river, and erected castles on their vessels from which to throw their missiles into the town, but the besieged made a second sally and destroyed the stockade, which was afterwards rebuilt and again destroyed. Meanwhile, the water in the river falling, the Japarese fleet was left aground, whereupon some Portuguese vessels were sent round and blockaded them on the strand. The Japarese then applied for terms of peace, which the captain of the fortress only agreed to upon such onerous conditions that they preferred to continue the siege, although both sides were now reduced to great want. It having come to the knowledge of the

* This river appears on the maps at S. Bâtu Pahat. Off its mouth is the Formosa shoal.

Captain of Malaccá that reinforcements, both from Japara and Achin, were on their way to join the siege, he sent out a small fleet to meet them. A battle ensued in which the Portuguese were victorious, but the Japarese who were before Malacca, finding that the Portuguese fleet had left the mouth of the river free, raised the siege and retired after a blockade of three months.

The King of Achin again appeared before Malacca, on the 31st January 1575, with a fleet of 113 vessels and a large quantity of heavy artillery. This time the city was not taken by surprise as on former occasions, it having been amply provisioned from Pegu and Bengal. There were, however, only three Portuguese vessels in port, which were sunk on the following day by the Achinese, and only fifty soldiers within the walls, most of the Portuguese troops having run away immediately after the former attack on the place by the Japarese. During seventeen days continued sallies were made against the enemy on shore, with the view of creating an impression that the Portuguese were stronger than they really were. The Achinese, not understanding these tactics, and fearing an ambuscade, raised the siege and retired.

It does not appear that anything further of great importance occurred in connexion with Malacca until after the commencement of the seventeenth century. In 1611* the Viceroy of India, Ruy Lourenço de Tavora, having received news that the Dutch were collecting and arming large fleets, with the object of making a descent on Malacca and China, sent orders to all the places and forts in the south to be prepared. This news would seem to have been premature, for it was not until August 1615 that any Dutch ships appeared off the city. Six vessels were sent out, and fought them until darkness came on and the enemy

* "Decada de Bocarro," T. I., pp. 98 and 388.

escaped. Although the Dutch had not apparently up to 1627 attacked Malacca, their rivalry in trade and the continued wars with Achin had reduced what had formerly been one of the most important and flourishing centres of trade, and one of the most valuable of the Portuguese possessions in the East, to a mere dependency.

MSS., Vol. A., 2—28.

On the 5th July 1629 commenced the famous siege of Malacca by the Achinese, who had nearly 400 sail and 20,000 men. On the 6th they fixed their batteries and commenced the bombardment. On the 21st October the Governor, Nuno Alvares Botelho, with 30 ships and 900 picked Portuguese, arrived at Malacca and at once engaged the enemy, whom he succeeded in driving off after very severe and prolonged fighting, on the 6th December, capturing a great number of the enemy's ships and guns.

D. R., Livro 33, fol. 249 vo.

From 1634 to 1636 the Dutch and Achinese combined to molest the Portuguese at Malacca, keeping vessels in those waters so that the ships of the latter could only get out with great difficulty, and the trade there was consequently completely paralysed.

D. R., Livro 34, fol. 39; Livro 39, fol. 9.

In a letter to the King on the state of India, dated the 30th October 1635, the Viceroy (Conde de Linhares) observed that the King of Macassar was friendly to the Portuguese, but hostile to the Dutch; he had taken the islands of Maluco and Amboyno, whose natives had defeated the Dutch, leaving them only their fortress of Amboyno. The King of Macassar had sent an embassy to Goa requesting the Portuguese to assist him in driving out the Dutch, and promising them a monopoly of trade there. The Viceroy was, however, unable to avail himself of this offer, owing to the want of forces to oppose the Dutch in the Straits of Singapore, where they were in great power. The Ambassador stated that the King of Macassar had provided a force to proceed to Banda, to cut down the nutmeg trees on that island, which, it was thought, would strike a fatal blow to the prosperity of the Dutch, who relied on this source of revenue to enable them to carry on their trade in India. The Conde impressed upon the King the importance of providing him with a sufficient force to defeat the Dutch, in which event, he said, the latter would be discredited and refused trade in those parts, since they were everywhere cordially hated, and only succeeded in carrying on trade by means of the forces at their command. He also desired to overawe the Dutch at Mataran, and to prevent them from coming to terms with its King. The King of Bantam had declared war against the Dutch, and had sent an Ambassador to the Portuguese offering them facilities of commerce. But the Achinese favoured the Dutch rather than the Portuguese. Communications with the King of Pegu had resulted in his opening that port to Portuguese commerce. In the following year the Viceroy reported (6th January 1630) that the Dutch had then blockaded Malacca with five or six vessels for over two years, during which time they had captured 14 ships from the Portuguese, besides others which they had forced to run on shore. Trade there was, consequently, greatly depressed, and it was further affected by the hostile action of the King of Achin.

D. R., Livro 35, fol. 300.

Antonio Van Dieman, the Dutch Governor General, in a letter to the King of Achin, of 7th June 1636, sent him presents of artillery and horses taken from a Portuguese vessel from Muscat. He had then eight large and other small vessels off the bar at Malacca to stop the Portuguese trade there, and he offered the King of Achin, if he would come with a large force to assist him, to take the fortress and city of Malacca,

D. R., Livro 40, fol. 298.

which he anticipated could be accomplished in a few days, as the city was in a deplorable condition.

D. R., Livro 40, fol. 375.

The President of the Danish East India Company (Bernardo Pessar), who was then on friendly terms with the Portuguse, informed the Viceroy, under date the 21st September 1637, that the Dutch were preparing to blockade Malacca, Ceylon, and Goa. In a letter of March 1638 the King pointed out to the Viceroy the great importance of Malacca, as it was, he remarked, only by the retention of that place that the Portuguese could hope to retain their trade with China and the south.

D. R., Livro 44, fols. 51 and 223.

D. R., Livro 47, fol. 16.

Early in the year 1640, news arrived in Goa of an impending attack on Malacca by the combined forces of the Dutch and Achinese, but the only available relief that could be sent was one galiotta. Before its arrival, however, it was reported that the Dutch had begun the the attack without waiting for the Achinese, and had blockaded the city with a fleet of thirty vessels. They were afterwards joined by the King of Pam* (? Pahang). The blockade of Malacca commenced at the beginning of August 1640. Very little information is given in these records of the progress of the siege, but it appears from them that the fort and city were taken on the 14th January 1641. An inquiry held subsequently relative to the loss of Malacca elicited the fact that this result was in some measure due to a quarrel between D. Diogo Coutinho de Oçem, Captain

D. R., Livro 48, fols. 76 to 90.

D. R., Livro 49, fol. 140 vo.

---

* In the *Lendas da India* it is stated that Pam is a port, city, and kingdom on the coast of Malacca, and that the King thereof used to be a friend of Albuquerque (T. II., p. 771). In the *Subsidios* this place is called Paham, and is described as a maritime city on the Malacca peninsula (pp. 5 and 6).

of the fortress, and Luiz Martins de Souza, Captain-General of the Fleet. The latter was captured by the Dutch and taken to Jacatara, whence he was subsequently sent to Goa, where both he and Diogo Coutinho de Oçem were imprisoned. The Viceroy, in reporting this loss to the King, suggested that one of the objects of the proposed peace with the Dutch should be, if possible, to obtain the restitution of Malacca, but, failing this, he urged that a new settlement should be formed in the neighbourhood, for which purpose he suggested the river of Formosa,* twelve leagues from Malacca, as a suitable site. Neither of these objects was, however, realized, and, with the year 1641, ended the Portuguese power in the Malay Peninsula.

D. R., Livro 48, fol. 76.

---

* *See* note on page 148.

PORTUGUESE INDIA.

SECTION VIII.

CHINA AND JAPAN.

According to Visconde de Santarem,* the history of the first Portuguese settlement in Macao is shrouded in a certain amount of obscurity. He had been able to find no authentic account of it in the Public Records in Lisbon, and I also failed to find any official statement of that event. The historians of Portuguese India relate that, in the year 1508, Diogo Lopes de Sequeira was instructed by Dom Manoel to proceed to Malacca, and from thence to make inquiries in China as to whether any foreigners were settled there; but the results of these inquiries have not been published. It does not, however, appear that between that date and the year 1517 the Portuguese had any direct communication with the Chinese.

When Lopo Soares de Albergaria left Lisbon, on the 7th April 1515, to succeed Affonso de Albuquerque as Governor of India, he had with him a fleet of 15 vessels, and was accompanied, amongst others, by Fernão Peres de Andrade, Antonio Lobo Falcão, and Jorge Mascarenhas, who were under instruction to proceed to China with the view of opening up a trade with that country. The Governor selected Fernão Peres to command in this enterprise, and he, accompanied by one Thomé Peres, started from Goa in February 1516. This expedition proceeded as far as

* "Memoria Sobre e Estabelecimento de Macau."

Pacem, when, finding the monsoons unfavourable to their further progress, they went back to Bengal. From thence they sailed to Malacca, and, leaving there in August, they arrived off the Bay of Cochin China, where they lay for several days, and then, as the winds were contrary, they returned to Malacca. Fernão Peres left Malacca again for Pacem, where he took in a cargo of pepper, with which he returned to Malacca, and starting thence again in June 1517, with seven ships, he made a fair voyage to the "Islands of China," and anchored off Veniaga,* which is 18 leagues from Canton. Three leagues from Veniaga was another island where the Admiral resided, whose duty it was to report to the authorities at Canton any arrival of foreign ships, and the nature of their cargoes, &c.

Here Fernão Peres met a large fleet of junks, and, having satisfied the Chinese Commander that he was bent on peace, obtained from him the assistance of pilots to navigate his ships to Canton, where he arrived in safety. Having anchored off the city, Fernão Peres sent Thomé Peres on shore as the King of Portugal's Ambassador, and he, having concluded a peaceful arrangement with the authorities, obtained from them permission to erect a factory on the Island of Veniaga. Fernão Peres remained at Canton till September 1518, on which date he sailed with part of his fleet for Malacca; whilst the remainder, accompanying some junks belonging to the Loo Choo Islands, proceeded to Ningpo, where they succeeded in establishing a factory, from whence they opened up a profitable trade with other parts of China, as well as with Japan.

It has been alleged by some that Thomé Peres suc-

* Tamáo, on the north-west coast of the Island of Shang-ch'wan, was a renowned harbour, to which foreign and Chinese merchants resorted for the sake of disposing of their respective investments. João de Barros and other historians designate it often by the Malay word Beniagá, or Veniagá, which signifies a mart or place for mercantile business.

ceeded in concluding a treaty of commerce with the Emperor, but no references to any such treaty is to be found in the Portuguese archives, and strong doubts exist as to whether it was ever made. At any rate, as the results of this Embassy, the ports of China were about to be opened to the Portuguese, when Simão de Andrade, a brother of Fernão Peres de Andrade, appeared off the coasts, and, pursuing the policy followed on the coasts of India, established a factory at Timáo (Shang-ch'wan), and built a fort there, in order to defend himself against the pirates, without having first obtained the necessary permission.*

On the death of the Emperor Wontsoung, the Chinese authorities had Thomé Peres de Andrade, who had been detained all this time in Pekin, reconducted to Canton, and orders were given for the expulsion of the Portuguese from that city. This led to a fight, in which the Portuguese were defeated. Some authorities state that Fernão Peres died in prison. Visconde de Santarem, however, says it is certain that he with twelve followers was liberated after undergoing torture, and then exiled. He married and died, according to Mendez Pinto, in 1548 or 1549.

By 1542 the Portuguese had already a considerable establishment in the city of Niampo or Liampo; and Japan is said to have been discovered in the same year by Antonio da Mota who, trading in a junk belonging to the port of Chinchew (about 100 miles south of Foochow), was cast by a typhoon on the coast of that

* Sir Andrew Ljungstedt, in "An Historical Sketch of the Portuguese Settlements in China," says of Simão de Andrade, "He built "a fort, and ended by arrogating to himself the prerogatives of a "Sovereign, venturing to condemn a sailor to death, and to have the "sentence executed. This act of open hostility, and the refusal to "withdraw from the island, filled the measure of his iniquity. A "Chinese squadron laid siege to the port. Simão would have perished "of hunger had not a strong favourable gale most opportunely arisen; "he took advantage of the accident, and escaped (1521) with three of "his vessels."

island. In 1549, the Portuguese established another settlement at Chinchew; and, in 1557, at the request of the Chinese, they obtained permission of the Mandarins to trade in Macao,* but not at any other port in the Empire, although they were still permitted to go to the fairs at Canton. In the years 1583 and 1585 the Portuguese in Macao obtained permission from the Viceroy of Canton to administer justice amongst themselves; and in 1587 the wealth of the Portuguese colony was so great that the place was named "Cidade do nome de Deos de Macao" ("the city of the name of God of Macao)."

From Macao there had sprung up an extensive trade with the Spanish Settlements in the Philippines, but soon after the union of the two Crowns this trade was forbidden, and the Portuguese settlers at Macao then directed their attention more particularly towards developing a trade with Japan.

It is stated by Bocarro that Christianity flourished in Japan in the year 1600, but that soon afterwards the Emperor commenced a system of persecution against that religion. In 1614 a law was passed expelling all priests and members of religious societies from the island, and foreign vessels were prohibited from landing there any

---

* There appears to exist a great deal of uncertainty as to the manner in which the Portuguese obtained possession of Macao, and the tenure upon which they held it. Some historians have stated that a celebrated pirate having seized upon Macao, blockaded the ports of China and laid siege to Canton. The neighbouring Mandarins having asked for the assistance of the Portuguese they went to the relief of Canton and obtained a signal victory over the pirate, and it has been alleged that, in consideration of this service, the Emperor of China bestowed Macao upon them as a mark of his gratitude. No mention is, however, made of this event by the more reliable authorities; and from the fact that the Portuguese had been settled at Macao some years before the pirates were driven from the Chinese seas, it is considered more probable that, as has been stated by others, the Emperor of China permitted the Portuguese to establish a trading station on the peninsula of Macao in consideration of the payment by them of "tribute or ground rent, and "duties on their merchandize."

more priests or friars. All converted Japanese were compelled to return to their original faith, and it is alleged that several Japanese Christians suffered martyrdom rather than recant. Reference is also made by Bocarro to William Adams,* an Engish pilot who was in Japan about the year 1600, who had been in Lisbon and spoke Portuguese. "He told the Japanese," Bocarro says, "that if they wanted peace they must oust the Spanish "and Portuguese from their territories."

The Portuguese had now firmly established their position at Macao, and they were anxious still further to consolidate it by the erection of a fort. Accordingly, on the 10th November 1610, the King, writing on this subject, cautioned the Viceroy to proceed in a peaceable manner, and at the same time to make presents to the Mandarins, and explain that the fort would result in great benefit to them. He also impressed upon the Viceroy that without the consent of the Mandarins in the matter, the trade in those parts would be in danger. Trade however does not appear to have flourished with the Portuguese here better than in India, for in a letter of the 28th February 1613, the King wrote to the Viceroy as follows :—

D. R., Livro I., p. 395.

D. R., Livro II., p. 341.

"The Bishop of China writes to me saying that affairs in Macao are in a very low state, so much so that even beggars cannot live there; the priests have received no money for some time and are, in con-

* William Adams went as pilot in a Dutch fleet which sailed for the Indies in 1598. His vessel got separated from her consorts, and with difficulty reached the coast of Japan in April 1600. Adams was sent to the Court of the Emperor, over whom he succeeded in obtaining a considerable influence, and when Captain Saris arrived there with an English fleet, in June 1613, Adams accompanied him to Court, and assisted in procuring for him the necessary privileges for trade. He subsequently accepted an appointment as second in command of the factory which Captain Saris established at Firando. Adams made several voyages to Siam and other places in the East India Company's interests, and remained in their service until 1616. After this he remained in Japan, where he died on the 16th May 1620.

sequence, unable to obtain the necessaries of life. As it is but just and right that these people should be paid, I charge you to see that payment is made to the bishop and clergy of all amounts due to them."

In this year certain Mandarins desired to turn the Portuguese out of China, and one of them sent the following complaint to Macao* :—

"I am informed that the Portuguese do not conform to our laws, and if they do not mend their ways we will have them turned out. If you wish to remain here in security you must agree to the following:—(1.) Not to introduce Japanese servants on penalty of death. (2.) Not to buy any Chinese natives, as directly you buy them you have their hair cut, and dress them in Portuguese clothes. (3.) Not to erect any new houses without permission. (4.) Any merchant arriving here who is single is forbidden to land, but must remain on board his ship."

In reply the Macao people declared that they would obey these laws, as they wished to live in peace with the Chinese.

In 1615, the King gave instructions for fortifying Macao, and directed the captain of that place to keep his plans secret, and to proceed with the érection of the fort. Should the Mandarins ask any questions he was to put them off with the answer that it was for their good, inasmuch as it was to protect the place against the continued attacks of pirates who infested the neighbourhood.

D. R., Livro III., p. 337.

Macao was attacked by the Dutch† in 1622, of which the following account is given in the Portuguese Records :—

Bibliotheca Publica MSS., Vol. B., 6–17, fols. 82–84.

"On the 29th May, when least expected, four ships (viz., two Dutch and two English) arrived off the bar of Macao, and gave a salute which

---

* Bocarro, p. 724.

† The following is the account given of this engagement in the India Office Records :—

The English ships took no part in this attack, although it suited the purposes of the Dutch to represent that they did; witness the following extract from a letter sent home by Richard Cocks from Firando, under date of 7th September 1622 :—

"The Hollanders this year sent a new fleet of ships of 14 or 15 sails, great and small, to have taken Amacau; but they had the repulse, with

could not be mistaken. Lopo Sarmento de Carvalho, who was not the man to be caught napping, hastily summoned all the people on shore and formed companies, and fortified the ports which were in a weak state. Observing that the beach of Cacilhas, distant from the city about a quarter of a league, presented an easy entrance for the enemy, a sand bank was erected to protect the shore. At night he embarked with eleven small craft and awaited the enemy. Matters did not come off as he expected, for the enemy left the next morning for the Island of Viados, to await the vessels from India. Perceiving the designs of the enemy, the prudent captain sent off in great haste seven well armed craft to convoy the vessels from India, in which they were successful, as they not only brought the Indian ships safely into harbour, but also some from Solor, Borneo, and Macassar. Matters remained in this position when, on the 21st June, 13 more Dutch ships arrived off the bar (nine larger ships and four patachos). On the 23rd June the enemy approached with two large ships carrying 25 and 30 pounders, with which they attacked the bulwark of S. Francisco from 2 till 6 p.m. The battle waxed very hot, but in the end these two ships were totally disabled. Firing ceased at night, when the captain went the round of the forts to cheer his men. The next morning, at daybreak, the enemy opened fire again, at the same time despatching a number of boats to the Cacilhas beach. Under shelter of their guns they landed 800 musqueteers, besides a great number of Japanese, who succeeded in

---

the loss, as some say, of 300, and others say, 500 men, and four of their ships burned; the king of China now permitting the Portuguese to fortify Amacau, which he would never condescend unto till now, and hath given order to the Viceroy of Canton to assist them with 100,000 men against the Hollanders, if need require. There was four of our ten ships of the fleet of defence, two English and two Hollanders, plying up and down before Amacau before the Holland fleet of 15 sail arrived there. The English ships were the 'Palsgrave' and the 'Bull,' who in passing by hailed them with a noise of trumpets, but the Dutch made them no answer, neither by word of mouth nor otherwise, but passed in by them with silence, which at first made them stand in doubt whether they were friends or no. But the Hollanders made account to have taken the town at first onset, without the help of our shipping or men, and therefore vouchsafed not to speak to them; yet failed of their purpose. But since have fortified themselves in an island near to Isla Formosa, called Isla de Piscadores, where they report is a very good harbour and water enough for the greatest ships in the world.

"The Hollanders have given it out to the Chinese that they are Englishmen, only to bring our nation in disgrace; of the which our China friends in Japan have advice, and have returned answer per two or three several conveyances to the contrary, and that we had two English ships before Amacau when the Hollanders gave the attempt against the place, but went for Japan without assisting them at all."—O. C. 1078.

capturing the intrenchments after a gallant fight. Seeing the Portuguese in full flight, the enemy pursued them and captured the first heights, the Portuguese still retiring. On reaching a place called Fontinha, however, three well directed shots from S. Paulo caused the enemy to halt. While this was taking place, Lopo Sarmento de Carvalho was, with the remainder of the force, some way off, but being informed that the enemy had captured the heights, he hasted to meet them, and joining with those who were retreating, arrived at the Fontinha in such good order that the enemy made for the hills. Sarmento was, however, too quick for them, as perceiving they were bent on capturing the hills on the eastern side, he marched from the western side, and gained the summit first. Here a fearful fight took place, and the enemy was eventually driven down with great slaughter. Three hundred of the enemy's picked men were killed, besides a number of those who were drowned in their attempt to escape. The Portuguese captured from the euemy eight standards, and over 500 muskets, swords, and one cannon."

D. R., Livro 33, fol. 247 vo.
" " 34, fol. 5.
" " 35, fols. 261, 267.

At page 33 reference has been made to the fact that, in 1635, the Portuguese Viceroy (Conde de Linhares), being in want of ships, chartered an English vessel from the President at Surat, for a voyage to China. That vessel was the "London," and the special object of the expedition was to fetch to Goa 4,000 quintals of copper and about 100 pieces of iron artillery. The "London" first went to Goa, where it took in a large cargo towards which the people eagerly contributed, selling even their wives' jewels to provide freight, in consequence of the greater security it would enjoy than if in a Portuguese ship. It was observed in a letter to the King on the subject, that this species of commerce was so nearly extinct that the people appreciated the opportunity to renew it "as if it were a general pardon." Two Portuguese factors were put on board, with orders not to allow any of the English to go ashore at the ports they visited, especially in China. Under a pass from the Viceroy, this vessel visited Malacca and Macao, and made observations of their respective entrances and fortifications. On arrival at their destination, the English desired to themselves petition the Mandarins to measure their ship, but this was frustrated by the Portuguese factors on board. They did some trade in China, and asked to be allowed to put up two thatched cottages for this purpose; they also desired permission to return to China the following year; and as an inducement for complying with this request they promised to supply drugs to the Chinese at fifty per cent. less than was charged by the Portuguese. Taking all these circumstances into consideration, Senhor Pero da Silva, who succeeded the Conde de Linhares as Viceroy, expressed an opinion that to have sent this vessel to China was the worst thing, in the interests of Portuguese trade, that could have been done.

D. R., Livro 41, fols. 191, 199, 200, 234.

At page 34, reference is made to the English fleet, belonging to Courten's Association, which visited India in 1636 under the command of Captain Weddel. These subsequently went to China, carrying with them a quantity of artillery, ammunition, and stores for the Portuguese to Macao. Captain Weddel had with him a letter from King Charles I. to the Governor General of Macao, informing him that he was sending Captain John Weddel and Nathaniel Montiney with the ships "Dragon," "Sol," "Catherine Planter," and "Anna," with special orders with regard to trade in the countries under the Portuguese. On arrival at Macao, the Captain General sent to enquire their business, to which they replied by returning letters from their Commodore and one from the king of England. Strict orders were given that no Natives should go near the ships, except such as the Captain General might send with provisions. As he could not prevent the Chinese from communicating with the ships, he sent to warn Captain Weddel to have nothing to do with them, as they were very treacherous. In spite, however, of all his efforts to prevent communication between the Chinese and English, the latter arranged with the Natives to show them the port of Canton, and to supply them, for that purpose, with two pilots, with whom they went sounding all round the islands at the mouth of the Canton river. A small patacho, employed on the same work, got close up to Canton and spent a month examining the coasts. On the 4th August the English fleet sailed for Canton, where they landed factors, money, and goods. The vessels were drawn up as near to the shore as possible, when the Chinese sent down some fire-ships with the intent to destroy them; in this, however, they were unsuccessful, and in retaliation, on returning, Captain Weddel bombarded and destroyed a Chinese stronghold. On the return of the fleet to Macao, the Portuguese sent an Ambassador to Canton, who succeeded in bringing away the English factors and goods. An attempt was made, by the Portuguese and Mandarins, to make the Admiral give an undertaking not to return to China to trade; but on second thoughts they came to the conclusion that it might be desirable to allow the English a limited trade there, on condition of their carrying Portuguese artillery to Goa from Macao, where it was cast in some quantities, in order to protect it from capture by the Dutch.

While these English vessels were at Canton, a protest was sent to the Admiral, by the authorities at Macao, against their having visited that island without any orders from the Portuguese King or the Viceroy. In this document considerable surprise was expressed that the English had gone to Canton without authority, that being a spot which the Portuguese themselves had never been able to reach in their own ships, and fear was expressed that the Chinese would, in consequence, retaliate on the Portuguese. Captain Weddel treated this protest with scant courtesy. In a reply, dated "from our vessels in the Port of Canton," he expressed surprise at its having been made, and declared that in spite of it, the English intended to continue their trade "'with blood and sweat' in a land which you confess "is not yours, but belongs to the King of China. No "time to write more as engaged on more important "business." A considerable amount of correspondence on this subject passed between the authorities of Macao and Captain Weddel, and there is a copy of a "Chapa" from the Aitaun of Canton regarding "four vessels of "barbarians, with red hair, from abroad, which having "arrived here went into the mouth of the Tiger."

D. R., Livro 43, fols. 4, 37, 39.

Captain Weddel, on returning from Macao with his four ships, met a strong Dutch fleet in the Straits of Singapore, which demanded of him whether he had anything on board belonging to the Portuguese. Captain Weddel refused to give up anything, and sounded to quarters, whereupon the Dutch allowed him to pass free. He then went on to Malacca and Cochin where he delivered his cargo.

D. R., Livro 34, fol. 39.

In an account of the state of affairs in India, the Viceroy, Conde de Linhares, writing to the King on the 30th October 1635, just previous to giving up his appointment, remarked that the King of Japan was persecuting the Christians there; and that Portuguese commerce with that island had been greatly facilitated by the Camara of Macao having guaranteed the debts of private individuals to Japanese, which amounted in the aggregate to over 200,000 xerafins. The Chincheos, he reported, had risen in China and defeated the Dutch, taking several of their vessels by surprise, and he expressed a hope that this would effectually put a stop to commerce between them.

D. R., Livro 34, fol. 41.
" " 35, fol. 285.
" " 36, fols. 161, 335.
37, fols. 415, 513.

In another letter of the 30th of the preceding month, the Conde de Linhares declared that it was then impossible for the Portuguese to carry on commerce with China which, he remarked, "is the only profitable trade in these parts," owing to the strength of the Dutch fleets in those seas and in the Straits of Malacca, whilst the alternate route through the Straits of Sunda was long, tedious, and dangerous. The Emperor of Japan had turned against the Christians, several of whom he had ordered to be burnt alive; and His Majesty threatened that if priests continued to be sent to his country, he would burn all the Portuguese ships that might arrive there, together with their cargoes. The Dutch continued their usual enmity against the Portuguese in Japan, and represented that they themselves were not Christians like the latter; and they offered that if these were turned out of Japan they would undertake to capture Macao from them. The Dutch were permitted, about 1636, to establish a factory in Japan. They also made war on China and were admitted to trade at Chinchew.

D. R., Livro 48, fols. 127 and 148.

Reporting on the state of India in 1643, the Viceroy remarked that Achin and all the kings of the South were against the Portuguese. Japan had closed her ports to them, and, so far as he could see, there was very little prospect of their being reopened. This was much to the prejudice of the city of Macao, for since the trade with Manilla was now lost, unless that with Japan could be reopened, Macao must die of inanition.

D. R., Livro 59, fol. 4.

In January 1644, an Embassy was sent to Japan by the Viceroy, but, on its arrival at Macao, the inhabitants of that place protested so strongly against it that it was forced to return to India. On the 30th April 1646, the same Embassy started again from Goa, and arrived at Macao on the 25th July. Leaving there on the 11th August, it was forced by stress of weather to put back and passed the remainder of the year at Macao. On the 8th July 1647 it once more started, and, on the 26th idem, reached the Island of Cavallos, in sight of Nagasaki. Every conceivable delay appears to have been thrown in the way of the Embassy in conducting its negotiations by the Japanese authorities, who endeavoured to get the Portuguese vessel into their power, which attempt was only frustrated by the astuteness of the Secretary to the Ambassador. On the morning of the 15th August, it was discovered that a bridge of boats had been thrown across the Straits in front of the Portuguese vessels with the view of hindering their retreat. On this bridge the Japanese had erected ten castles, some of which were armed with artillery, and about 2,000 vessels also appeared on either side of it. A letter from the Emperor was now delivered to the Ambassador, reminding him of the prohibition against Christians going to Japan, and calling upon him immediately to retire. The Ambassador inquired whether, if his King promised to refrain from preaching the Christian religion in Japan, the Emperor would then agree to terms of friendship, to which His Majesty replied that every moment he more and more prohibited any intercourse of his country with the Portuguese. After several other fruitless attempts by the Ambassador to come to terms, he was ordered to leave, and, accordingly, on one day the bridge of boats was opened and the Ambassador retired, without having accomplished anything, and returned to Macao.

On the appointment of General of Macao being conferred upon Dom Braz de Castro, in March 1648, he declined to go on the grounds that the city was completely impoverished, and the people in a state of revolution, they having recently murdered their late Governor in the streets. He considered it useless to go there without men or money, and there were neither of them forthcoming, since the Viceroy excused himself from sending any force there on the plea that the Dutch might consider it a rupture of the armistice.

In 1649, the Viceroy reported that commerce was

beginning to be opened up with the Tartars,* who had captured Chinese provinces down to Canton, when it was put a stop to by a Native of the Chinese dynasty appearing, who was immediately recognized by seven provinces. War ensued, accompanied by a plague, which in Macao alone killed 7,000 persons, mostly Chinese, and this effectually put an end to commerce there.

Tratados, T. II., p. 194.

The treaty of peace concluded between the Portuguese and English on the 10th July 1654 gave the latter permission to trade with all the ports in the Portuguese dominions in the East Indies, Guinea, the island of St. Thomas and other parts of Africa, but Macao is not mentioned therein.

After this date there appear very few important references to Macao or China in those Records which I have searched, and, from the absence of any specific

* The incursion of the Tartars into China here referred to was the insurrection of the Mantchous against the Chinese Emperor, which took place at the commencement of the seventeenth century. In the wars that followed, it is reported that, on one occasion, the Chinese emperor employed Portuguese artillerymen whom he brought from Canton. In 1638, there appeared in the field eight several armies, or corps of insurgents raised in different provinces by chiefs, each of whom usurped the title of king; two of these subsequently agreed to divide the country between them, and one of them marched upon Pekin, which he captured after a siege of three days, whereupon the Emperor, in despair, hanged himself, and with him ended the dynasty of the Mings. This occurred in 1643. The conqueror of Pekin did not, however, long enjoy the fruits of his victory, for he was shortly afterwards defeated by the Mantchou Prince Chin-che, who made a triumphant entry into that city and had himself proclaimed Emperor. Two of the sons of the last Ming Emperor were decapitated by the conqueror, but the third son escaped, and having fled to Nankin, was proclaimed Emperor there; he was, however, soon afterwards captured and strangled by the Mantchou invaders. Two other blood relatives of the late Ming Emperor were subsequently proclaimed Emperors by the two provinces Tche-Kiang and Fokien respectively. These were, however, speedily subdued, and on the capture of Canton by the Tartars, on the 26th November 1650, the Mantchou dynasty was firmly established in China.

details relating to later years in Portuguese works on the subject, it would appear that such trade as survived the events above narrated was carried on at Macao apart from any exciting, or other events of importance. That trade was, no doubt, greatly interfered with when the East India Company succeeded in establishing a regular commerce with Canton at the beginning of the 18th century.

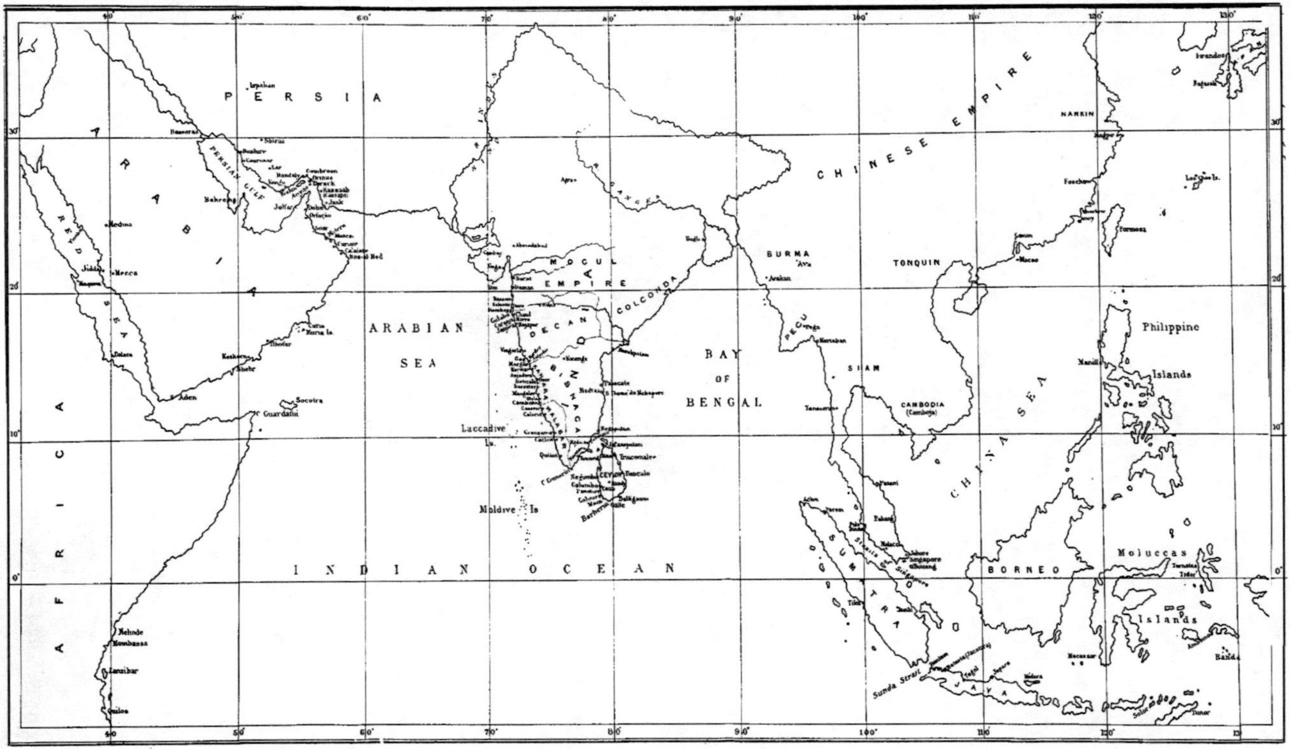

PERSIA
ARABIA
PERSIAN GULF
RED SEA
ARABIAN SEA
AFRICA
MOGUL EMPIRE
DECAN
COLCONDA
BISNAGA
BAY OF BENGAL
INDIAN OCEAN
BURMA
Ava
Arakan
PEGU
SIAM
CAMBODIA (Camboja)
TONQUIN
CHINESE EMPIRE
NANKIN
CHINA SEA
Philippine Islands
BORNEO
SUMATRA
JAVA
Moluccas
Islands
Formosa
Macao
Sunda Strait
Laccadive Is.
Maldive Is
CEYLON
Isfahan
Bassora
Bahrein
Julfar
Ras-al-Hed
Medina
Mecca
Jiddah
Aden
Socotra
C. Guardafui
Melinde
Mombassa
Zanzibar
Quiloa
Agra
Banda
Timor
Tidor

INDEX.

Page